THE BRE.

By Julia Dean

© Julia Dean 2021

Index

1	Chapter One: The Vision
9	Chapter Two: The Big Day Dawns
20	Chapter Three: Life at the CJ Memorial Hospital
31	Chapter Four: 'Settling in at the Charley J'
41	Chapter Five: One Year On
58	Chapter Six: A learning Process!
69	Chapter Seven: The Importance of Friends
80	Chapter Eight: An Unexpected Change of Direction
86	Chapter Nine: Moving On
95	Short Stories
97	A watery End
102	Khozi Bay
105	The Moon Man
107	A Heart Stopping Time
110	I Am Found
116	Thanks

CHAPTER ONE

The Vision

"Julia, get your head out of that book and do some work!" My mother was calling me and I knew better than to ignore her!

Little did I – or she - know then that my love of reading was to shape a very major part of my future life.

I lived with my mother, older sister Cynthia and younger brother Michael, in a two-bedroomed rented cottage in the pretty little village of Coaley, in Gloucestershire. I was born in December 1940, a war baby, and my brother two years later. Dad was not considered fit enough to be called up during the war, so was using his engineering skills in the Listers engines factory, but tragically died of a heart attack at the age of forty-three. Following my father's death my mother needed to work, and so she was taken on at Listers Factory, to weave industrial belts. The management there realised the desperate situation that she was in as a widow with three children under the age of twelve, and suggested that she did the work at home if they could set up the loom in the cottage. This meant that she could look after us during the day and weave the belts at night. She was paid according to how many she could produce! Life was hard for my mother, and money was always in short supply.

In our early years my siblings and I went to the Primary School in the lower part of the village near the church and vicarage, and the Post Office/shop. We walked the two miles to school each day, whatever the weather, and often across the fields, with the farmer being very gracious to us! We enjoyed it, and it built strength and stamina into us plus a love of nature, and an appreciation of God's Creation.

My parents had been brought up in the traditional Church of England faith and had sent us to Sunday School and Church each week. The demands of my father's work and his health problems meant that they were not very regular church-goers, but they joined us for the main festival events of Easter and Christmas. At Sunday school each year we were given books as a reward for good attendance. We loved these books because we only received such gifts on birthdays and/or Christmas during the war years, and I loved reading. I believe that it was through that Sunday School's reward system that I was, at the age of eight, given a book that would have an enormous impact on my future life. That book was *"On the Edge of the Primeval Forest"*, by Dr Albert Schweitzer, and it described his work in a hospital in Kenya. It opened up to me the picture of a country very different from our own, and it filled me with a vision, a desire to do similar work in that country when I was old enough to do so.

My teenage years, however, were rather dull in comparison with most. When I was fourteen my mother accepted an opportunity to move to the City of Gloucester to live and work.

The move to Gloucester meant that, due to our ages, my brother and I were sent to the only school that was able to take us. This meant that my teenage life was full of work, teenage social life somehow passing me by. Yet it was work that was meaningful and enjoyable so I didn't feel deprived! We settled into the school very quickly and, under the loving expertise of the teachers there, I thrived as never before. I found myself being awarded many certificates for different subjects, and eventually had the great honour of becoming Head Girl! This opened the door of opportunity for me to take up an offer to attend the local Technical College several days a week, in preparation for becoming a 'Blue Girl', at the Gloucester Royal Hospital. Through this I learned about all the supportive services of Hospital Nursing life, and this in turn could lead to an application for training as a State Registered Nurse. It was like an apprenticeship, and it served me well in mission life. Was my childhood vision coming into being?

The next step.

In preparation for the vision to be put into action I needed to train as a State Registered Nurse (S.R.N.) and Midwife, and I was able to do that in my home city of Gloucester. I first spent two years in the position of Staff Nurse and then Second Sister on the busy gynaecological ward there. During that time I was blessed with a good working and social relationship with a Dr Celia who was on the same ward. One morning she came on duty hugely excited, giving me news that she was leaving to respond to a call for doctors (by Anthony and Margaret Barker) at a mission hospital in Zululand, in the Republic of South Africa. This was distressing news for me as we had become friends and formed a working bond which I valued highly. However, she was so excited about her future journey that it brought my own vision more sharply into focus.

I continued to work hard, focused on widening my nursing experiences. I undertook midwifery training by completing six months of academic and hospital-based work in Cheltenham, Gloucestershire, followed by six months of District (community-based) midwifery practice in York. Still inspired by Dr Schweitzer's work in Kenya, I continued to pray that the Lord would open more doors of opportunity. On completion of these requirements and now a fully qualified Nurse/Midwife practitioner, I felt ready to apply for preparation for missionary work in Africa. And at last, an exciting invitation!

I was invited by Dr Celia to consider joining her in South Africa at the Charles Johnson Memorial Hospital, at Nqutu, in KwaZulu-Natal. The proposal struck a chord deep within in my spirit, and I felt that this could lead on to later opportunities for work in Kenya. As I prayed about it I felt led to approach the Anglican Missionary Society, The United Society of the Propagation of the Gospel (U.S.P.G.), to apply for Missionary training and financial support. The society responded favourably to my application, inviting me to meet up with them at their headquarters in Tufton Street, London. They advised a period of six months Bible College preparation in Birmingham at the College of Ascension, an Anglican Convent, prior to final acceptance of me on a 5-year contract which would include the return journey payment to the country of their choosing. But they would consider my request for South Africa and Kenya in their discussions!

So when the time came, I resigned from my much-loved position on the 40 bedded Gynaecology Ward in Gloucester and headed off to Birmingham. It felt as if I was already travelling to another country as, apart from my brief sojourn in York ,I had never been out of Gloucestershire except for school summer holidays with an aunt and uncle in Shropshire with my younger brother Michael and older sister Cynthia. Thankfully the period of 6 months District Midwifery experience in York had added a little confidence to someone my mother had often referred to as shy and timid. However, my first impression of the College of Ascension was one of relief and joyful surprise on seeing the beautiful buildings and gardens. The latter had a wide grassed walk at its centre leading my eye to the distant horizon beyond the lovely herbaceous flower borders on each side. This was to become my 'Meditation Walk' each day, a special spiritual place for the 6-month training course. I have a vivid memory of the peace and beauty of that walk as, with others on the course, we reflected and meditated on what had been taught and what we had received.

On the first evening we were told that part of the convent disciplines was to keep silence from 9pm until 9am, including during breakfast, where we all sat together at long trestle tables. We soon learned that we were dependant on our neighbours to see and offer whatever was required for our food and drink. This could be a frustrating experience, but one which developed in us a conscious awareness of others' needs before our own, a skill which is of immense help in fostering good relationships throughout the journey of life.

One of the people I met at the college, and with whom I quickly became friends, was Barbara Picton. She was on a different course but we socialised together whenever we could. Rebellion at the Silence Rule was setting in for a number of us so we made plans to go out for an evening of Ten Pin bowling at a nearby venue. We had a most enjoyable evening and returned to the college in good spirits chatting away beyond the 9pm Silence Rule. On arrival at the front door however, we found it locked and as none of us felt confident enough to ring the bell, we looked for another way in. One small transit window had been left open so the group looked to me, as the smallest person, to wriggle through, once they had hoisted me up to reach it. All was going well until a cold voice of authority from above said: "Do you wish to get in?" At this point all who were with me 'forsook me and fled' leaving me halfway through the window trying to extricate myself from my belt which was holding me fast on the window hook!

Following this humiliating and embarrassing experience, sleep did not come easily to me - this was not the behaviour of prospective missionaries in training! The following morning, I made an appointment to meet the Mother Superior and apologised for what had happened. I suggested that perhaps I did not have the necessary qualities to be a missionary and I was therefore willing to withdraw my application and return to nursing. She responded with kindness, a hint of humour, and Godly love, informing me that in fact the college was soon to close following our group completion of the course. Headquarters felt that the college was no longer able to effectively prepare potential missionaries in a changing world society, and it was their intention to upgrade the buildings to be more appropriate for male and female attended courses in the future. She then advised me to speak with the relevant person in London to seek the way forward.

I went to that meeting with some trepidation, but at that meeting I was surprised and delighted to be offered a place as a Nursing and Midwifery Missionary on a 3-year (not the usual 5-year) contract. This was because, at the age of twenty-three, I was the youngest missionary they had ever sent overseas. They were concerned that I would miss my family too much in a different country with only the Mission for relational support. The other joyful surprise was that the contract was to be in South Africa, at the Charles Johnson Memorial Hospital where my friend Dr Celia was still working.

However, there was one final hurdle! A 'commencement of contract' date of 6th August 1964 was set, and arrangements were made in South Africa and the UK ready for my departure. But towards the end of all the preparations a vital South African permit, required to enter the country and travel to the Bantu area, failed to arrive. The disappointment was tangible and felt by all, except perhaps my family who were glad to have my presence with them for a while longer. Urgent letters from officials were exchanged until finally the permit arrived and the date was rearranged for November 1964.

CHAPTER TWO

The Big Day Dawns: November 26th 1964

Am I ready for this?

The day of departure arrived. I was feeling excited and daunted at the same time and also a little sad. A large group of family and friends had gathered to see me off. My mother, brother Michael, Connie Smith (my senior gynaecological nursing sister and friend), Ann Lane (another nursing friend) with her little daughter Debra (my God-daughter) and Valerie (another friend living with us at the time). We all set out in a hired minibus for Southampton where the ship was docked.

The weather was cold and bleak as one would expect in November, but it brought back memories of a trip earlier in May that year when a group of us had said farewell to my sister (Cynthia) and her husband (Frank) at Liverpool docks when they emigrated to Canada on the beautiful liner, the Empress of Canada.

We arrived at the docks safely, everyone trying to be positive and happy, laughing nervously and holding back the tears at this moment when we were so unsure of what lay ahead. We were all wondering when, or even if, we would ever see each other again.

It was in that state of mind that I boarded the huge Union Castle liner - the Stirling Castle - to the cheerful sound of a brass band and loud roars from the crowds who had come to see the great liner and who were throwing ticker tape. This helped to raise my spirits after the tearful farewells. And so it was, along with hundreds of other passengers, that I climbed aboard the ship, making my way to Berth 1 and my allocated cabin, number 548, a small space next to the ship's engines with no portholes - hot, stuffy and smelly. I couldn't help wondering, was this a foretaste of how missionary life would be?!

I then went up to the Berthing Level of the ship to get some fresh air, and at 7pm I returned to the cabin to find a beautiful bouquet of pink carnations and yellow chrysanthemums, a gift from my family. And there was still one more surprise - I was joined by another passenger, Joyce Willoughby- the small cabin had shrunk even more! We welcomed each other and soon learned that close fellowship is to be valued, even if it needs to be worked on!

At 4pm the beautiful ship pulled anchor and majestically departed from Southampton docks. Her two masts, streamlined red funnel with black top and lavender grey below, were a grand sight and

The Stirling Castle

the dockside crowds responded with cheers, clapping and waving flags and anything else they could wave before turning away with tears to return home without their loved ones.

In my diary for 1964 I recorded some basic details, plus highlights of the trip.

Friday 27th November, First Day at Sea

Slept well last night in spite of the ship rocking and rolling as we went through the Bay of Biscay - a route notorious for rough passages. The ship has taken on a heaving rhythm but the stewards keep telling us how fortunate we are that the seas are so calm. I am not convinced! It is only with great mental effort, prayer, and heeding advice to stay up on the top deck for fresh air and keep my eyes fixed on the distant horizon that I begin to find my sea legs.

Joyce and I venture down to breakfast to find we are the only ones there. I ask the dining steward if we are too early for breakfast. "No", he replies. "You are the only ones to appear so far because of the rough sea!" Then we notice that the table edges have been put up to stop the cutlery and china falling off. Joyce and I look through a porthole and see huge waves. We move away quickly.

Saturday, 28th November

Enjoyed a dance last night and today saw a film called **The Moon-Spinners** *which was also very enjoyable. As children* *in a post-war culture in our village, we had not been able to go to the cinema, due to cost and lack of availability, so I decided to reclaim some of my lost childhood and go to the cinema with films for the young people on board. There I caught up with such films as Donald Duck, Ivanhoe, the Secret Garden etc. Great fun.*

In the evening, Joyce and I attended the Captain's Cocktail Party. Glamour was everywhere, not part of my social lifestyle prior to this journey, so initially I felt quite awkward. The handsome but rather sarcastic Purser took our names and announced us. We shook hands with the Captain. His warm, gentle and encouraging manner made us feel accepted, valued and worthy to be there.

The official photographer took our photographs as we were shown to our seats for a four-course dinner followed by a dance up on the top deck in the lovely warm weather.

Sunday, 29th November

Today we docked in Madeira. We had seen the beautiful, volcanic, craggy island as we approached. Nearing the harbour, we are amazed to see young people diving into the water to pick up coinage which had been thrown in by passengers who had travelled this route on previous occasions. Local traders also come to meet us in their rather precarious looking small boats.

The dark, suntanned, Portuguese-speaking people catch the ropes from the ship, looping them through the waiting baskets enabling them to be hauled up on board. At 3.30pm a ferry takes us to the pier where we encounter many beggars, and sleds pulled by oxen with tinkling bells. Other lovely sights are vividly coloured flowers, reds, yellows and blues, flower girls in national costumes, lacemaking, stalls laden with handmade sun hats, sandals, skirts and handbags. My only regret is that my finances do not allow me to contribute much to these lovely, welcoming people who apparently struggle with the widespread poverty. We return to the ship which will sail later this evening.

The rest of the voyage follows a basic routine of food, frolics and fun! I fear that my waistline will certainly suffer, in spite of the availability of plenty of exercise - deck quoits, table tennis and other similar games.

Tuesday, 1st December

Very hot today. At 10.30am we went to the Navigation Bridge where we were given an interesting tour of all the equipment.

Thursday, 3rd December

The Aquatic Sports Event took place today, great fun, particularly the 'greasy pole'. A large, black ,tarred ,round pole was placed over the width of the swimming pool, smeared with grease and 2 crew members invited to sit astride the pole. They then hit each other with a cushion. The winner was the one left on the pole when the other fell into the pool. Onlookers, cheered and clapped encouragement for their chosen crew member!

Friday, 4th December

Today the 'Crossing the Equator' ceremony took place. The ship's officers dress up as Neptune, court ladies, a physician and nurses. Victims are led to the 'Court', charged, and sentenced to the ducking stool, which throws the victim backwards into the swimming pool.

Wednesday, 9th December

We have reached an area where two tides meet, the Atlantic and Indian Oceans, now the Cape of Good Hope, but better known by sea-farers as the Cape of Storms (Cabo das Tormentas), as named in 1488 by the Portuguese explorer Bartolomeu Dias. Quite a few people have sea sickness as a result but a farewell dinner has been enjoyed by most with plenty of champagne, wonderful food, and dancing.

Thursday, 10th December

Cape Town approaching! Excitedly get out of bed at 5.00am to see my first glimpse of the much talked about Table Mountain. Sadly, it has low cloud covering the top, referred to as 'the tablecloth', I'm told. What a disappointment! And

I am unaware that we have sailed close to Robben Island where, I later learned, Nelson Mandela was imprisoned. A sobering thought that, as I was arriving in Cape Town, he was going into prison. Little did I know at that time how his name and life issues would be brought into my awareness over the next few years and what a mixture of joy and sadness would result from following the events unfolding before us in those troubled times of apartheid history.

We dock in Cape Town at 6.45am. There are an amazing number of people here to welcome their relatives to Cape Town. However, before contact can be made, we have to complete the obligatory customs forms which are proving to be difficult and confusing. I have received a note of welcome from a person called Mrs Long who intended to meet up with me. Eventually we do meet up, following an exploration of the immediate area with my ship friends. We find the "Whites Only" signs quite shocking, a taste of what apartheid is all about.

Friday, 11th December

Around the Cape towards Durban. We set sail again at 1.00am for the next stage of the journey to Port Elizabeth. The atmosphere seems to have changed since we left Cape Town. Why is this? Is it linked to fewer people, new people, new expectations, all impacting on relationship dynamics? We are nearing our final destination and there is a growing insecurity as we anticipate leaving the safety and routines of the 'Little Ship' which has been our world for a while. I note the change but make the decision to look forward to the next developments, whatever these might be.

It had been suggested that we look out for whales in the cold waters around the Cape but we are not blessed with their beautiful presence on this occasion. As we progress up the coast towards Durban, we are told that the waters are now warmer and will be favoured by sharks. We look out for these but, again, do not actually spot them. However, just looking out for these legendary creatures gives an excitement all of its own.

Port Elizabeth appears to be all uphill and I do not find it a pretty place. It resembles a shanty town from a distance. We take a tour around the city, including a visit to a Snake Pit. It seems that there are a great number of potentially dangerous snakes in the country; this is not the time to dwell on this bit of information, I decide!

The beaches of Port Elizabeth are lovely, as are the flowers - Canna Lilies, Poinsettias and the famous Jacaranda trees. A place called Happy Valley proves to be most attractive with its herbaceous borders each side of a grass walkway.

In the evening we attend a carol service organised by St Mary's Anglican Church. The choir has evidently been in existence since the 18th century and has an excellent reputation for the quality and high standard of its singing.

We are delighted with the choir's inspirational performance and return to the ship with much improved thoughts of Port Elizabeth and a desire to return, one day, to explore further its history and beauty spots.

Monday, 14th December

We arrive at the port of East London and go ashore to the beautiful beach but avoid swimming in the sea in view of the earlier warnings of the possible presence of sharks.

Tuesday 15th December

Our final ship destination. We arrive in Durban docks, three hours late. The customs officials are as helpful as they can be, but I am in a state of anxiety when they go through my suitcase to see what reading material I have packed. Black Beauty - is it about a horse? They also question me about an accompanying bale registered by U.S.P.G., my 'sending' Mission. This contains medicines, clothing and medical utensils and has been listed in the official papers I am carrying. I hand over the key and list of contents to the officials but wait in the customs area for more than two hours. I realise I have missed my scheduled train and am the last person left with the officials. I am hungry and tired and burst into tears. At this the officials become unexpectedly concerned and send for a female immigration official who *takes charge, arranging for me and the bale ($4.75c customs duty paid) to board a train leaving for Glencoe, Natal.*

I feel great relief and thankfulness for the kindness of the official who came to my assistance. Once on the train I experience a relaxing and very beautiful journey in the luxurious comfort of a 'Whites Only' compartment. Aged only twenty-three and in a strange country, this feels good, and I am aware that it would be so easy just to accept the situation in order to feel, and be, safe. But I can't help wondering how God must feel about the situation?

Wednesday 16th December

Finally, arrival at the Charles Johnson Memorial Hospital.

At 11.00pm I step onto the platform at Glencoe, in Zululand (now KwaZul-Natal). There are two people there to meet me, one young man the hospital secretary, Victor, and the other young man, Jeremy (Dr Barker's nephew), the current engineer at the Mission Hospital. They are charming in their welcome and my introduction to the last stage of the very long journey. In spite of tiredness, my senses register that the night sky is full of stars in an extremely black background - beautiful. It is also very cold, due to the area being 5,000 ft above sea level.

We travel the 40-mile dirt road in the hospital ambulance Land Rover to Nqutu where Drs Anthony and Margaret (Maggie) Barker, and Maggie's sister, Phyllis Newton, welcome me into the warm kitchen heated by an Aga Range Cooker. I shall never forget the moment of meeting Anthony and Maggie, dressed in homemade 'Wee Willie Winkie' hats and nightshirts with paraffin lamps in their hands!

Part of their introductory welcome was Anthony's booming voice saying 'Jules, the good news is that you have arrived safely. The bad news is that the only job we have for you is that of a midwife! We have waited until you arrive to give you this news because we had heard you might not come if you heard this before leaving England! We understand that you hated the midwifery training experience and had said that you never wanted to have anything to do with it in the future. However, we have a plan which we will tell you all about in the morning'.

With that I am shown to a small bedroom in the house where I am more than ready to rest. The next day I will begin to try to settle into this amazingly different culture, but at the same time there are some panic feelings at the prospect of having to put my very recent midwifery training into practice after all! I can only trust in God...

CHAPTER THREE

Life at the Charles Johnson Memorial Hospital

Thursday, 17th December 1964

M y first day at the Charley J. (as it was affectionately known as!) I was awoken by a blast of music - Beethoven's 8th Symphony - coming from Anthony and Maggie Barker's flat at the opposite end of the corridor. This turned out to be a daily occurrence. It was Anthony's routine to rise at 4.00am and write short, precise but meaningful letters in his beautiful, calligraphic handwriting, and I was one of the people blessed to receive these letters over the years. Appreciation of the daily musical feast was not always shared by others but for me it was yet another aspect of life in this fascinating adventure I had embarked upon.

After the simple breakfast and prayers led by the Barkers we attended the Holy Communion service in the large church at the centre of the hospital grounds. This served the local Zulu community as well as the hospital patients and staff. As a British Anglican, used to hushed reverence and 'order' during such services, here was a strong, eager, joyful expectancy of the Lord's presence, and priority was given to exuberant praise and thanksgiving before, during and after the service. The Zulu men and women loved dressing up in special robes and lavishing incense to the point where the interior of the church was full of smoke. At the conclusion of the service they all went out to their various duties with beautiful, harmonious singing and dancing. What a way to start a working day!

Comprehending the Anglican form of service in the Zulu language was a new and lasting challenge for me but I learned to love the musical rhythms (resembling the Welsh language) of saying the Lord's Prayer each day. The presence of Anthony and Margaret Barker taking leadership in this was a great encouragement to us all.

After the morning service the doctor's ward round took place. The hospital chaplain would be part of this so that he could respond to the spiritual needs of patients who had very mixed ideas of who God was. However, they recognised a power beyond themselves and cried out for help in times of crisis, of which there were many. The Zulu population was mainly of tribal tradition with an allegiance to local witchdoctors, a major problem for the Christian leaders who prayerfully and practically battled the many outcomes of Zulu medicine and enemas which too often killed the little children the Zulu parents loved so much.

In many ways it was a battle that could never be won by the hospital. The Zulus often made comments such as 'the hospital medicine did not work, they killed our child', or 'our child lived because of the *Muthi* (medicine) of the witchdoctor'. The Barkers told me they had struggled with this attitude for most of the 30 plus years they had served in the Charles Johnson Memorial Hospital, but they tried not to let it discourage their faithfulness and love for the people.

Instead of the usual ward round I was shown the existing maternity unit where I was introduced to two British, recently retired, midwives who had just undertaken an 'across Africa' journey in a Land Rover. They had deliberately wanted to visit the Charlie J. Hospital to see for themselves a method of caesarean section performed under local anaesthetic, which Anthony Barker had learned and perfected to suit the needs of the women and babies in the absence of resident qualified anaesthetists. The technique also got around the difficulties in obtaining the relevant gases in remote rural areas.

This procedure had evidently been learned from Professor Hugh Philpott who was based in Rhodesia at that time. He became increasingly more involved with the hospital over the years, sharing his obstetric and midwifery knowledge and numerous practical skills. These were of immense value to the Barkers and to the maternity unit development.

The two British midwives, Miss Lois Beulah and Miss Barbara Brierley, had been extremely experienced leaders in midwifery professions in London hospitals prior to their retirement. When they had heard of my forthcoming arrival and my aversion to midwifery practice, they had offered their services as my guides and mentors for a 3-month period to give me support and confidence. They were not allowed by the South African Nursing Council (some of whom they had previously taught!) to do any practical, hands-on midwifery because they were retired, and therefore not legally covered if anything went wrong. However, they could be in uniform and instruct me as to what needed to be done.

The following turned out to be their real objective, which Anthony and I gratefully accepted. The plan was to demolish the existing, wood-and-tin roofed labour shack and construct a new, purpose-built, maternity wing with five labour wards, an eclamptic ward, 96-bedded postnatal wards, a ground floor specialist unit to accommodate 15 premature babies, and a hall for 100 pregnant mothers!

My inadequacies in the light of all the challenges set before me now loomed large and I readily acknowledged that help and support was going to be crucial. There was no room for professional or personal pride here. I took a first step towards learning humility!

Having met my tutors, I was shown around the maternity unit which I referred to as 'The Shed'. Earlier in the day approaching the unit, my eye had caught sight of the old door with a crack in it from top to bottom through which cockroaches were running in and out. The door opened into a small, poorly lit, hot and airless room accommodating eight low beds. There was just enough space between each bed for midwives to kneel and examine the women in various stages of labour prior to moving them into the delivery room. These beds were also used to treat women suffering pregnancy complications such as raised blood pressure (pre-eclampsia), eclampsia, (fitting state), bleeding in pregnancy (ante-partum haemorrhage) and premature labour. The potential for constant noise and distress was obvious to any visitor.

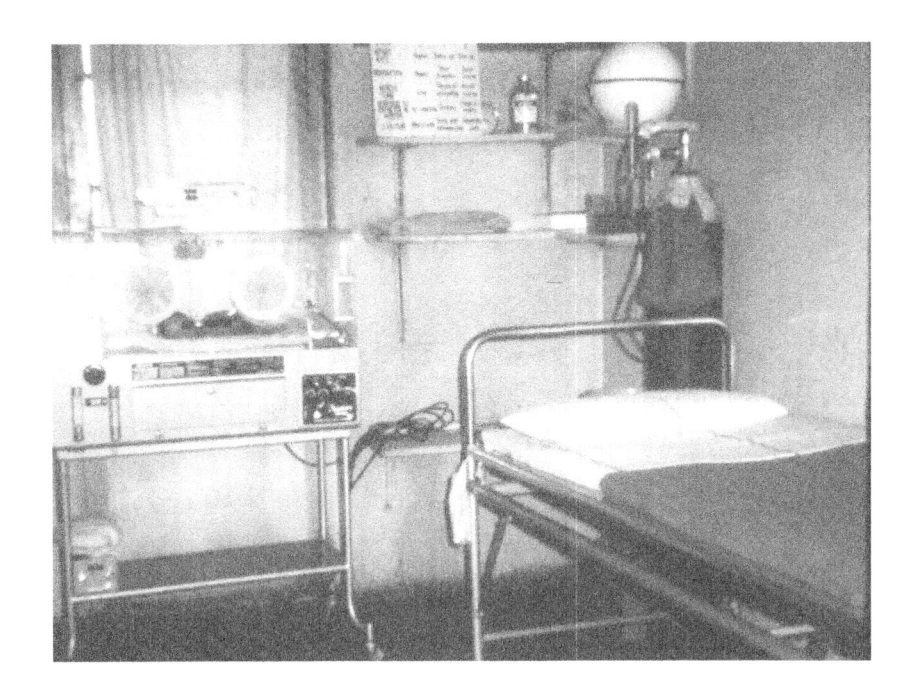

Just adjacent to here was the delivery room. It had one small window and was so narrow that it was only able to accommodate a three-quarter length ex-dental/delivery bed which had lithotomy poles at the end. These were essential if the labouring mothers needed assistance to complete delivery such as forceps (rarely used here) or ventouse (vacuum extraction) – the latter was the preferred and the safer option I was told.

Behind this bed was a tall, black oxygen bottle which I later discovered was empty and some rubber tubing which was beginning to crumble. This did not boost my professional confidence. On enquiry, I was given the explanation that supplies of this nature were extremely difficult to maintain in remote areas such as this one, so 'do not depend on it'!

Around the other two sides of the room were flat-topped paraffin stoves on which were placed green wooden, apple style, boxes in which the tiny premature babies were nursed.

Some were only one pound in weight. They were dressed in hats and jackets made of 'gamgee' material, (cotton wool covered in soft gauze mesh) and were fed with their mother's expressed breast milk by glass pipettes or teaspoon.

From this room a doorway led into the sterilising area known affectionately as 'The Black Hole of Calcutta' because the walls and ceiling were covered in a greasy, black substance - the result of constant steam and pollution from an upside down paraffin stove. The stove was used to boil the one and only set of steel instruments in a fish kettle, and these were required for each delivery! It was a small comfort to me that I was familiar with such a stove from my childhood days.

Where were the neat, surgically cleaned, light and wonderfully equipped Midwifery Units I had left behind in Britain? Being faced with this scenario was both shocking and overwhelming to a newly-qualified British midwife and I couldn't help wondering what the mortality and morbidity figures might be.

Following the tour of the unit I was asked if I would consider helping Maggie Barker's sister, Phyllis Newton, run a midwifery training school by teaching practical 'hands on' skills to the students in the unit each day. This would release time for her to focus on the academic side of the 2-year South African nursing course which had to be completed in the English language. The implication of this was that I would not have the opportunity to learn Zulu, essential for good social and professional communication. However, although this should obviously have been be a priority for me, the students' needs had to take priority in order for them to be academically successful as auxiliary midwives.

I was then called over to an ancient, rat-infested wood-and-mud hut where Sister Monica Mncube was about to deliver a local woman's baby. It was thought that I might like to see the delivery.

Sister Monica was a greatly experienced, professionally trained, local midwife of advancing years. Well respected, she possessed great wisdom and humility, and gave a sense of security, encouragement and comfort to everyone who came into contact with her. The baby she delivered with ease was a delicate shade of pink; only the presence of dark brown at the base of his tiny nails and a head of black, curly hair revealed his Zulu heritage. His lusty cry announcing his entry into the world reminded me that I was witnessing another miracle of life, another tiny new life made in the image of God. What a beautiful moment to see my first Zulu baby born in this day of so many surprises - not all of which had been uplifting up to this point!

So much was happening. I had met the two tutors, received a large amount of information concerning the development plan and had had the request to help Phyllis, so now I was given time off to unpack, settle in and mentally process all that was rushing through my mind.

This included the disappointing news that Dr Celia, my friend who had worked with me on the M1 Gynaecology Ward in Gloucester, would not be able to greet me personally after all. She had met an American doctor at the hospital, had fallen in love with him, and was going back home with him to get married! However, both felt that they would return to the Mission in the future and they would meet up with all of us then, and this gave me some comfort!

A pile of letters awaited my arrival, which was even more comforting, and they helped to reduce the emotional impact of the reality of family and friends being thousands of miles away. I realised that I would need to set aside time on a regular basis to respond to all who had pledged to support me in various ways during the 3-year contract. Included in the list was the vicar of my home church, Rev Hugh Potts, who had prayed a protective prayer for me during the final Sunday morning service prior to my departure from Britain. He had also undertaken to send letters of encouragement and church news updates during my absence.

I did not, after all, unpack completely because it appeared that my mud hut was almost ready for me to take up residency, following a repaint. A felt excited at the thought, though at the same time there was some anxiety about thatched roofs, spiders and other unknown possible occupants. I decided that it was better not to enquire about such things at that time, perhaps ignorance was bliss! Instead, I went for a walk around the hospital grounds to explore my new environment. The beauty of vibrant reds and the orange colours of canna lilies delighted me, along with the colours of the wild verbena, dahlias, gardenias, and the blue colour of the few jacaranda trees that people had told me to look out for. Evidently Pretoria (the seat of government) is famed for the beauty of these trees in season. The warm air was heavy with the fragrance of the flowers, and I become aware also of the high-pitched sound of crickets in the background. This sound, I discovered, interfered with one's ability to speak the letter 's' during a conversation. It made for some interesting conversations!

Returning to my 'mud hut', I discovered that further surprises were in store. I had received an invitation to the medical theatre to watch Dr Barker perform various surgical procedures that were on his operating list. The operating theatre was part of a planned extension to the hospital and was built in 1955, between two wards with its door opening straight onto the passage linking them. There were two frosted windows, opening onto the back of the building, which provided the only ventilation for its occupants. There was also a small extension to allow sterilisation of metal instruments by the use of metal baths heated up on the top of triple headed Primus stoves. Unlike most operating theatres in the U.K. this one was dark, small, airless and hot - no air conditioning here! However, these 'trifles' became insignificant as I watched this truly gifted man perform a prostatectomy, followed by an iridectomy and numerous minor surgeries and biopsies.

He was being assisted by one of the newest medical students. These students came from all over the world (many from London) to experience for a few months the amazing life in this Mission Hospital. I was told that many returned later in their careers to serve for several years in their professional capacity, and this had proved to be vital for the ongoing development of the medical, nursing and district work of the mission.

I left the theatre enormously impressed by the enthusiasm of Dr Anthony as he taught his assistant all the required procedures, to the obvious awe and respect of the young man, who was being given opportunities under the master's guidance to participate in surgical ways not afforded to him in his home training country.

A final highlight of the day for me was yet to come. I had been told that the electrical power for emergency surgery and for pumping water from the nearby dam was supplied by a Lister Engine. This information brought special comfort to my spirit, as I remembered that the Lister engine was from Dursley, my home town, and that my deceased father had worked in the factory as an engineer during the war. What a lovely ending to an amazing day!

CHAPTER FOUR

Settling in at the 'Charley J'

Friday 18th December 1964 - My 24th Birthday!

This birthday was being celebrated away from the familiarity of home - no loved family members to hug, kiss and sing Happy Birthday. But at least I had two cards, one from U.S.P.G. and one from a close friend, Ann Lane, which lifted my spirit. However, I also became aware of a sore throat and cold symptoms which quickly developed into a severe chest infection. I was instructed by Dr Maggie Barker to stay in bed, take antibiotics and rest for the week. What a way to start a 3-year contract!

During this time, I received quite a few visitors and was shown acts of kindness from people I had not previously met. There was a bowl of fruit from Dr and Mrs Newton, who were in their 80's but still working. Mrs Newton supervised the Sewing Room where all repairs of hospital garments took place and new ones were made, at the request of the various departments. Dr Newton ran the Pharmacy, a highly responsible position where no mistakes could be made without the risk of dire consequences. These two people were hugely respected and loved.

Victor Spencer, the hospital administrator, also visited, bringing his transistor radio and a large book of 'funny stories' to cheer me up. He turned out to have a unique sense of humour, to which I responded with enthusiasm. I was deeply touched that such a young man would show such kindness to a newcomer, but Victor continued to be a loyal, faithful and challenging friend and was very specially used by God in the mission.

On returning to health and work duties, I was happy to respond to the Chapel bell being rung to call us to one of the twice-daily Anglican services and twice-weekly Holy Communions in the chapel of Christ the King. This building was in the centre of the hospital grounds and was large enough to serve both the hospital and the local community. Attending these services became a familiar and enjoyable event. The Zulu staff and the local community clearly loved the services, particularly on special feast days when the church leaders robed up and we processed around the hospital grounds. The singing by these naturally gifted Zulu people was wonderful and I was spiritually fed by their enthusiasm, musical skills, and reverential worship - even with the overpowering use of incense!

Following one of these services, my eyes were drawn to observe the hospital title, large white letters on a green background - Charles Johnson Memorial Hospital. So who was Charles Johnson?

I discovered that the hospital was established by the Anglican Church in memory of Archdeacon Charles Johnson, archdeacon in the 1930s. Archdeacon Johnson had been ordained in 1887 and later moved to nearby Masotsheni where, by the time of his death in 1927, he had established 40 parishes, each with its own church. He had been a greatly loved man in the community, highly respected for all that he had established in the Lord's name, so the completion and naming of the new hospital, built under Dr Barker's leadership at Nqutu, was a fitting memorial.

Prior to this the hospital was little more than a clinic with seven beds. It had not expanded due to the drought conditions, even though it was near to the Blood River at Rourke's Drift, the scene of the Zulu/British war. Following the construction of a dam, the original hospital was moved from Rourke's Drift to Nqutu, five miles up the road. This had been a wise decision. In December 1964, when I arrived at the hospital, the number of beds had increased from seven to 700, with numerous buildings to serve the needs of both staff and patients. The construction of the dam had potentially provided sufficient water for the hospital's increasing medical demands and supportive services.

However, the area remained vulnerable to extreme drought conditions and was very dependent on rainfall. We had one memorable 6-week period early in my first year, when a single bowl of water was used to…

- bath a baby
- wash the mother

- clean the bedside locker
- clean the bed and mattress
- clean the floor

This was for us a valuable lesson about **not** taking water for granted, **not** complaining about rain, and recognising fully our dependence on water resources for laundry and other services. As a result, we used to pray more earnestly for rain. Each day during the summer season these prayers became more real and passionate. When the sky revealed the approach of a heavy thunder and lightning storm, daily between 4.00 and 5.00 pm, we would rejoice. In addition to supplying our needs the visual beauty and sound effects were spectacular in themselves and the heavy downpours of rain brought clean refreshing air. These were times of wonder, joy and profound thanksgiving for God's provision.

The Staff House at the Charley J was the main welcoming place for all new arrivals and visitors. It was a very important psychological and physical resource for supplying the basic needs of food, warmth, fellowship, security and a feeling of being 'at home'.

Mama Gladys Hlatshwayo was in charge and did an excellent job of looking after us all. Some of the foods, however, were not unanimously loved – for example, the glutinous, lumpy, cooked mealies - the staple diet of local Zulus. Life depended on the availability of them so everyone grew them, after which they were stored (away from rats) and cooked 'on the cob', boiled or crushed for daily consumption. However, they lacked essential nutrients which gave rise to Kwashiorkor (protein deficiency) and general malnutrition in the children (Marasmus). More tasty and nutritious foods such as mealie meal porridge, vegetable curries, olives and mulberries were always welcome.

Curries would sometimes be supplemented with gravy, goat meat, chicken or, at special community celebrations, beef. These meals would be planned for any type of celebration and would be exciting and fun, everyone working together to provide the vast amounts of rice and mince or stew required for several hundred people. Any excuse to relax, get to know each other, socialise, sing and dance, Zulu and Scottish style, was welcomed! As long as it was on the Mission property, we were not transgressing any apartheid rules and we made sure that we kept to a strict finishing deadline so that the local village residents' sleep was not disturbed.

Nevertheless, we always ended such events with an enthusiastic rendering of the African National Congress Anthem 'Nkosi Sikhalel iAfrika' - God bless Africa.

25th December

I return here to my diary entry for this special day and the exciting days to follow:

Christmas Day, my first in South Africa and the first away from home. It is very hot; however, we still have a traditional British Christmas with all the trimmings. The staff have been making decorations and presents every spare moment for weeks.

Where did they manage to get a turkey from in this very remote place on the map? We have had a wonderful time celebrating Christ's Birth throughout the day in spite of it being extremely busy in all the wards. At some stage the Christmas Story was enacted out by our Zulu colleagues, the most excellent singing and drama performance I have ever experienced.

And next, moving day!

The big day has arrived. We move into the purpose-built Midwifery Unit - what a joy for all of us but particularly for the Barkers and all the staff who have initiated, planned and built it long before I stepped into the picture.

We all work hard as a team, happily doing the tasks set before us, aided by the gentle, harmonious, singing of the nurses and midwives. The presence of the two London tutors is especially valued today. Each day they have come to the unit dressed in the S.A.N.C. uniform of white dresses with maroon belts and epaulets plus white starched caps and have verbally guided me with gentle assertiveness and authority to carry out what has needed to be done.

This practice has transformed my academic head knowledge into realistic, practical skills, as well as broadening and deepening my understanding of how to manage this rapidly developing and busy midwifery unit. I will need this once they have departed from the mission. Their vast collective experience and wisdom has been reflected in guiding us as to the best places to put items in order to avoid having to move it all again later on.

The first move is for the antenatal mothers to take up residence in the large hall. There are no fixed furnishings, the floor mattresses being placed by the mothers themselves following their invitation to the unit on the basis of potential high risk labour problems. They are normally accompanied by the 'aunties' - extended family members who help to care for the pregnant woman while she waits during the two-week period prior to birth. This will include feeding themselves, so there have been a few difficulties getting agreement as to where to site a kitchen sink with running water for the washing of utensils. We can only hope that all will go well.

The move to the labour and delivery rooms is taken more slowly as we have to ensure that the mothers and babies are kept warm during the transfer from the old, overheated unit to the large light and airy one. Additionally, everything has to be ready to respond to any emergency event during the move. We have been unexpectedly busy in the old unit recently so there are labouring women on the beds and under the beds on extra mattresses.

Five babies are born during the night and another one is safely delivered soon after the day duty midwives start their shift. However, the mother then has a large haemorrhage which necessitates intravenous rehydration therapy by Dr Anthony Barker. Happily, all is well with mother and baby, to everyone's relief.

Soon after there is another emergency, where I discover that the baby's head is not descending into the mother's pelvis as one would expect in the presence of good uterine contractions. The baby is in a posterior position (the baby's back in line with the mother's back) so that the head is not being propelled downwards into a flexed position to enable it to rotate and be delivered normally. Both the mother and baby are beginning to show signs of distress so we need to assist the mother by either a caesarean section or a ventouse extraction. The male-shaped pelves of the Zulu women usually does not allow the use of obstetric forceps as there is too little space to insert them without danger, so Dr Anthony performed his first ventouse extraction, thankfully very successfully. The baby is smaller than we had anticipated but in a good state of health following the procedure, which brings much joy to the mother and everyone else.

Gradually, as the day progresses, order replaces the chaos of the morning. We begin to see the emergence of longed-for space, privacy for women in labour and post-delivery, babies in proper cots swinging from the end of each mother's bed, and with adequate toilet and washing facilities, and in clean, light and airy wards.

At the end of this very special day, tired emotionally and physically, we gather together as a team (and with a number of others on the mission) to reflect on progress and to share in a well-earned cup of tea, cake and prayers of thanksgiving for what has been achieved so far.

I take this opportunity to show some of my photographic slides of the old empty, tin-roofed mud and brick shed which has served faithfully for many years as a place of obstetric and midwifery life-and-death events. It will be demolished in the next few days and take its place in history, one with honour and respect for all those over the years who have served the Lord in caring for the local Zulu people. As we are reflecting on this, we receive the joyful news that Dr Maggie, who is away in Johannesburg having surgery herself, has come safely through major surgery, is recovering well and hopes to be home soon.

This is a special blessing on a special day, particularly for Anthony as he has missed her so much. Lovely news for me as well as Maggie had sent a sweet note to me saying 'keep the place on the boil, dear one, until I get back!' A big responsibility in her absence but a comment which has lifted my resolve not to let her down.

An official blessing of the new unit took place at a later date. This was a good time of thanks and rejoicing for God's provision of money, people with the appropriate skills and a team of supporters and prayer warriors to bring the vision into reality.

Our 'Angel Midwives' have moved on to the next phase of their journey, but I shall never forget their patience, good humour, humility, necessary rebukes, wisdom, and above all, the sacrificial and unsalaried giving of their time and professional teaching skills, which gave me the confidence to continue the work alone when they had gone.

I believed that the Lord would bring His blessing in His way, in His time and for His reasons to these lovely women. And so we at the 'Charley J' were delighted when, at a later stage, we received news of Lois being awarded an OBE for her services to midwifery in the UK. We rejoiced in this news but at the same time felt that they both deserved a medal for their services to us in South Africa and hoped that this would happen at some stage. A letter from Lois in April 1965 told me that she and Barbara were to travel in the May of that year to Cape Town where, she wrote, "I have to go to pick up the OBE and a glass of sherry". I was invited to join them for the event, but circumstances prevented the joy of that. Duty prevailed!

CHAPTER FIVE

One Year On: A Reflection

It is unbelievable that a whole year has passed! Time has moved me through periods of suspension, followed by acceleration, as the days of learning, absorbing, reflecting, experiencing challenges in mind, body and spirit begin to integrate me into the flow of the 'ethos' of the Charlie J community.

Sometimes it feels like only yesterday that I sailed from Southampton, at other times 'tired old missionary' comes to mind! It's in those latter moments that I recall the words of a leading Anglican vicar who said: "Please do not return home looking like an old-fashioned missionary"!

This memory would stir me to dress up in something really feminine such as a lovely pair of gold and white brocade trousers and jacket sent as a birthday present from my sister. The response from black and white colleagues was: "Let's have a fashion show", which is exactly what we did. A focus for celebration is welcome in remote places like this and the sharing of food always appreciated even if it is 'left overs'. Proverbs 15:17 says, "Better a meal of vegetables where there is love than a fattened calf with hatred".

As I reflect on this year, I feel that my professional midwifery and management skills have advanced greatly. I realise now that my earlier fears and unspoken criticism of the maternity unit's mortality and morbidity figures were poorly founded. It had been producing excellent statistics in spite of its 'shed environment' and now, since moving into the new maternity unit, was increasingly doing so.

The years of the loving, patient and faithful care of the auxiliary midwives, under the deeply committed and highly professional leadership of Dr Margaret Barker, had proved to be a real safeguard. She had produced a programme of care focused on reducing the risk of infection for the premature babies, infection being the main killer of these tiny, vulnerable infants.

Under her programme, only the mother was allowed to handle her baby. The mother would be encouraged to stay in the unit until the baby was strong enough to go home and would be taught to feed her baby with her own expressed breast milk or pooled, sterilised, breast milk from other mothers, with the aid of a teaspoon, tube or glass pipettes, until the baby was able to suckle at the breast and gain weight.

No formula cow's milk, or feeding bottles were allowed in the unit as experience had shown that infection resulting from badly sterilised bottles was the main killer of these babies. The mothers did not have the money to buy bottles, sterilising fluid or the artificial milk on a regular basis in order to maintain the nutrition for the baby over a long period; they would try to stretch resources by adding a teaspoon of powdered formula milk to a bottle of water which may not have been boiled properly. This resulted in gastric infection, dehydration and death.

Malnutrition could be a less serious, short-term outcome but, if not corrected, led to great suffering and premature death at a later stage of the baby's life. Breast feeding for two years prior to weaning had proved to be lifesaving in the area. The well-meaning but stubborn insistence of companies trying to sell their formula products to the hospital and to mothers outside the perimeters of the mission was an ongoing problem.

As Maggie and I worked together in the maternity unit, I became more aware of the responsibilities she carried. She headed up the care of the Paediatric wards, where there was a constant flow of very sick children being admitted to the unit. Sometimes - too many times - two or more children needed to share a cot. These little ones were admitted for life-giving correction and management of protein deficiency problems which caused swollen, oedematous bodies (Kwashiorkor), Marasmus (a general lack of basic nutritious food), caused these children to be thin, miserable and prematurely aged, through constant hunger. As a result of these two main problems the children often succumbed to other diseases such as Dysentery, Measles and Tuberculosis.

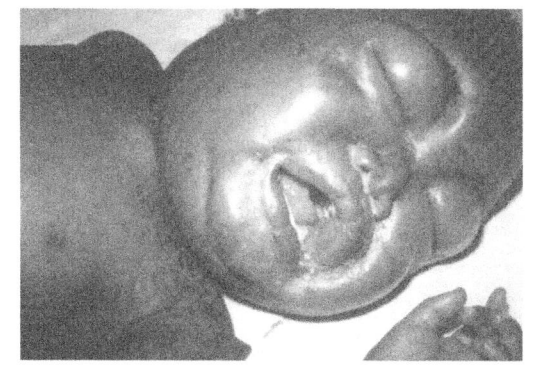

The suffering of these children brought great distress to Maggie, particularly when death took them, but she would pray for the situation and then carry on. She took on overall care of the entire Mission Hospital while her husband Anthony was sorting out problems out in the remote areas. In these cases people were unable to access the hospital services due to the terrain, or physical or mental disability. However, Maggie left the surgical problems, including caesarean section, for Anthony to carry out as he was the designated surgeon, holding the qualification Fellow of Registered College of Surgeons, with the specialist skills to deal with each procedure safely.

Building relationships within the mission community.

A request was made by the Zulu domestic staff for a knitting class in order for their already substantial artistic skills to be broadened. The people in the Natal area were well known for their beautiful beaded and crochet work. They produced beaded hair pieces, necklaces, bracelets, belts, pregnancy aprons, shields, and milk utensil and food protective covers. They also made the cooking pots for everyday use but these also were beautifully shaped as well as practical. Sadly, they were fragile when it came to trying to transport them any distance.

Those of us who knew how to knit, gathered together with those who wanted to learn, about twenty in all, and met regularly.

Progress was quickly made but the advantages in learning and progressing skills were overtaken by the joy of sharing in friendship and fellowship. Singing always accompanied such gatherings, as did sharing our cultural diffcrences, learning English and Zulu languages and cautiously exploring current apartheid news and how it affected us as individuals. In the latter case we needed to exercise caution as we were warned that "walls have ears", and "enemies can be within the camp".

As we continued to meet together, we realised afresh that these occasions were precious, as were the Saturday evening Scottish Dancing and the Sunday afternoon Rounders ball games! I am not a natural at ball games but even I was encouraged by Anthony Barker's booming voice calling out: "Come on Jules!"

There was also a request to start a Sunday school class. Earlier in the year one of the student midwives and I had taken toys, pretty flowers and relevant reading books, with pictures, to the children's wards. This had helped to introduce them to who God the Father was, Jesus the Son and His love for them, and aspects of His character.

The children seemed to be enjoying the teaching and, as many of the children suffered from tuberculosis, they were likely to be at the Charley J on a long-term basis. We prayed that the teaching would bring some comfort and hope into those little lives which had been blighted so much by malnutrition and subsequent illness.

Leadership and relationship learning.

About a hundred people were under my leadership as midwife in charge of the maternity unit. Comparing with the British system, our Zulu auxiliary midwives needed to complete two rather than three years of a less academic/more practical training course in order to gain the State Registered qualification that was roughly equivalent to the British qualification. However, the requirement of completing their studies in a different language from their mother tongue, (that is, English or Afrikaans), was for most a major obstacle for them to overcome. More importantly, the rules of apartheid did not allow a black person to have the equivalent of my leadership position, even though they might have completed the same professional midwifery training course as their white counterparts.

It was a mark of the Zulu midwives' grace that I never felt any resentment directed towards me on a personal level. We were able to share and discuss the knowledge of such injustices, without hostility, within the relative safety of the mission hospital's professional and social boundary setting. The exception to this was local telephone use which we were told was constantly being listened to by "others".

The midwives had responded well over the years to Anthony and Maggie Barker's great respect and love for all who came into contact with them, a good foundation on which to build, and I reaped the benefit of this. Money and salary was an issue but was never really discussed between us. At that time missionaries were usually given their travelling fare to and from the mission, plus an allowance of about 20 Rand (£10) a month and free food and accommodation. The Zulu midwives would have received a State Salary but probably not at the same level as their white colleagues.

Their good-natured question to me from time to time was: "Does your salary go straight to your family in England?" My belief was that they could not accept the truth that a white missionary working in the hospital, in any position, would only receive an allowance. This was understandable since they were so painfully aware of the material and financial advantages denied to them simply because they were born black. They both witnessed, and experienced the disadvantages for themselves, sometimes with emotional, spiritual and physical cruelty. Their understanding of this unfair regime unfolded as each day passed, challenging all of my preconceived thoughts and revealing to me the inadequacy of my knowledge regarding the life journey that I'd embarked upon.

We had determined not to practice 'Rules, Regulations or Attitudes' within the mission, but this was challenged on occasion. One example of this was in situations where I would correct students on a professional matter and the response could sometimes be: "Is it because I am black?" I would respond with a repetitive and sadly, not always patient, reply of: "No, it is not because you are black but because I want you to be able to work in any midwifery practice to the highest quality of care anywhere in the world". This response, together with praising and encouraging the good practice, calmed what could have been a difficult moment!

Long professional working hours, responding to the many medical emergencies arriving on our doorstep, being called out at any time of the day or night, was demanding and exhausting, but we were totally committed to serving our mothers, babies and team members as best we could, knowing that at all times we had the Lord's help and strength.

A season of change.

During my first year there were a number of changes. We had been greatly blessed by the midwifery skills of our oldest Zulu midwife, Monica Mncube, who oversaw the care of the Antenatal (waiting) women. It appeared that out of respect for her age and years of experience no Zulu mum-to-be ever dared to be disobedient when Sister Monica was about, for there were plenty of jobs to be found for naughty girls!

We were sad when the time came for Sister Monica to leave us - her husband had to retire from his job in Johannesburg. He had visited his wife twice in the year, as did all non-white men who worked in the gold mines of Johannesburg. This brought a bumper crop of new babies nine months later! Regrettably, they also brought with them infections such as tuberculosis. The living conditions in the mines were often cramped and unhealthy under the apartheid regime. This was distressing emotionally and physically for the men, but also for the women, as their husbands often brought sexually transmitted diseases such as syphilis back to them. This could then infect the baby in the womb, so most would need to be treated with antibiotics.

In Sister Monica's marriage there had been a faithfulness to each other over the years and it was with great joy that she was able to receive her husband home for a well-deserved retirement and enjoy a normal relationship, denied them under the Separate Development Policy Laws. We were delighted to have the opportunity to honour them with a Service of Farewell with much pomp and ceremony.

However, whilst we mourned the loss of some colleagues we rejoiced at the arrival of others. Dr Jon Larsen and his wife Jackie came to join us in February 1965. We found them to be a delightful couple who won our hearts very soon after their arrival.

I had the joy of getting to know Jon in his role as obstetrician in the maternity unit. His professionalism, breadth and depth of knowledge, practical experience, integrity, humility and deeply caring attitude towards all has been inspirational and a practical witness of his Christian faith. He was asked by Phyllis

Newton, Maggie Barkers sister, if he would give midwifery lectures to the students, to which he readily agreed. I asked if I might join them whenever possible, so that my knowledge base might be improved along with theirs. He and Phyllis had agreed to this, and I was greatly blessed in doing so.

The original plan – for me to manage the maternity unit and assist Phyllis Newton in teaching the two-year midwifery course – had gone well. The arrangement appeared to suit all of us but 'could be improved for the students' if the setting of State Examination questions was introduced. This was a comment from Phyllis to me, with the question, 'would I be willing to take on this additional task?'

Having considered this request carefully, I realised that it would be time consuming and a theoretical challenge for me, as I still felt the need to learn more about Zulu midwifery. Personally, I was struggling to master the Zulu language with its different clicks required with the tongue for the letters C, X and Q. My attempts and constant mistakes brought forth joyful laughter from the sweetly encouraging students, who now knew what it was like to struggle in writing and speaking in a foreign language for study purposes. However, the additional task of setting of State Examination questions would add to my knowledge, skills and confidence, and that would be hugely beneficial. Also, the students needed to improve their ability to answer the questions in English if they were to be successful in their final State Examinations. They had to be given the priority in the situation, and so I willingly took on the extra work and with empathy.

In this year also, another change, this time in the form of a very welcome material resource. We received our first Premature Baby Incubator. This came as a gift from wonderful fundraising friends and midwifery colleagues in the Maternity Hospitals of Gloucester and Cheltenham and from my church of St Catherine's in Longlevens, Gloucester, led by Rev Hugh Potts.

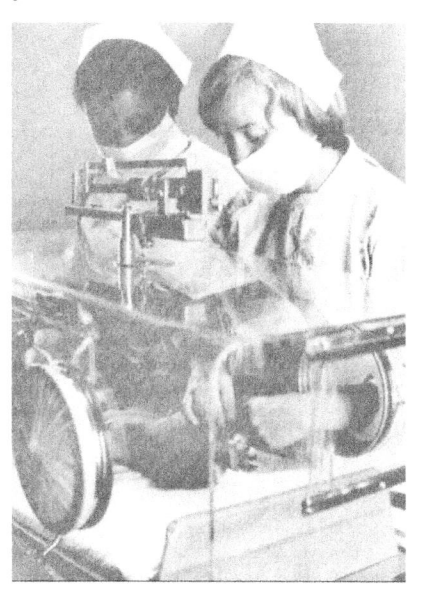

Although our little premature babies did well in their separate two-cot, half glass, cubicles, there were some who simply would not survive without the assistance of these especially designed machines. We were extremely grateful to all our donors who had contributed time, effort and finance to make this prayer request a reality for us. When the incubator arrived it was immediately put into constant use. Before that we had needed to borrow an incubator from the Batavia Mission Hospital in Dundee, 40 miles away, a loan initially promised for three months, but with grateful hearts retained for nine!

Life outside the Mission.

During my first year I learned more about my surroundings. The small town of Nqutu, of which the Charley J Mission Hospital is a major part, is 5,000 ft above sea level, a rocky, stony and drought-ridden terrain, hot in the day and cold at night. Flat-topped acacia trees, blue gum trees, prickly pear cacti and various types of aloes all thrive here, bringing wonderful fragrances and beauty to us throughout the seasons. At times the hillsides look as if they are on fire when the aloes are in full crimson flower.

Zulu homesteads are scattered around the hospital area. Set in circles of fenced-off land, the buildings and enclosure are known as a Kraal. Villages are not traditional but began to emerge as a result of the Apartheid Separate Development Acts of Government. This had included the forcible moving in of Black Townships without local consultation and with no apparent planning for supporting infrastructure such as water and sanitation. This inevitably resulted in typhoid outbreaks, fatal for many already weakened by malnutrition, poverty and extreme stress.

The dome-shaped houses within the Kraal enclosure are built by each family, usually by the women. The structure is a mixture of mud and dung with either thatch or galvanised iron roofs, no chimney, so smoke from the fire in the middle of the house fills the interior and escapes through the small entrance area. The Zulu residents usually have brown-coloured eyes as a result, and chest infections. The latter, plus overcrowding and poor diet, often leads to tuberculosis.

The Kraal has a surrounding fence of mud or sticks to protect the household and livestock. Animals such as cattle, goats and chickens are valued as revenue, gifts at special celebrations and tribal events. Historically, Zulu women were 'bought' and an open hoop, thick metal bracelet was put on the woman's wrist when an agreement for marriage had been reached. In more modern times this has been replaced by a request for cattle. The name used for such an agreement is the Lobola. Polygamy is normal in this area, so when reaching out to these people we needed to be aware that converting to the Christian faith could be a real stumbling block for them if insensitively handled.

The centre of the Kraal is the gathering place for the wives to cook over an open fire and for the children to play. The system appeared to work well until the local brew was consumed in large quantities! The hospital would then become rather busy with the victims of domestic fights between the number one wife and the others or the husband and his wives. The stitching on of torn ear pieces, head wound repairs and the occasional fatal stabbing or brain-damaged person was always a source of frustration and sadness to all involved.

Building relationships outside the Mission.

Locally, one large store was owned and managed by a white man, providing basic foods for local people. It supplied essentials including mealies and mealie flour and also hardware items such as galvanised buckets and roofing materials – a useful place to have nearby. It also sold clothing, including the very delicate, floating gauze and beautifully coloured scarves which the Zulu women bought to cover their hair and shoulders.

A pub, owned and managed by a couple called Mr and Mrs Drew was a favourite meeting place for the local white residents including those at the Mission. On Wednesdays, after the operating list was completed, Dr Anthony often invited his assistants to the pub for a drink in order to refresh themselves. This also served as a social outreach to the local white residents - a gesture by Anthony to build good relationships in an area where everyone recognised their need for each other, at some time and for a particular reason, in order to bring a good outcome for all, including the Zulu people we served.

Nqutu had a local, mainly white, population - people who had made their financial living from the Zulu geographical area, for example, by setting up and running the local food and hardware stores. Other people had been placed there, such as the Police and Prison management team and the above-mentioned managers of the public house.

The most intimidating building was the police station, with its own prison cells. Activities of all kinds and all people, were monitored at all times. The Mission was under constant surveillance by the police including, at night, from a four-wheel drive vehicle, the glowing end of a cigarette butt being a give-away. Telephones were tapped, hospital white people were restricted to walking on the main dirt road for recreational purposes, and occasional night raids took place, without warning, in order to try to find apartheid-breaking rules being breached through reading materials.

I was warmly welcomed by all but with a cautious, introductory exploring of where my political heart lay. Working in a Mission Hospital as a white person, I was viewed with some suspicion and as quite hard to accept, particularly by the Afrikaans policeman and his wife with whom I became friends. They taught me a great deal about how they grew up with anti-Black views, taught and nurtured from their earliest childhood years by family, friends and the prevailing society.

We exchanged robust conversations and probably never managed to convince each other as to who was right. They were patient and gracious with me and my British views. We also all had the understanding that we needed each other in this remote place, perhaps on opposite sides of the political fence, but in crisis situations of safety, health, childbirth we all did what we could to support each other. Dr Barker in particular was able to exert assertive measures for good in his role as Prison Medical Officer.

In our leisure time, the Tennis Club was enthusiastic in recruiting people from the mission. I was thankful to be included, a younger additional member to their small group, even if not wonderfully skilled. We shared in short local walks and visits to a small library, and enjoyed 'sundowner drinks'.

Three of us from the Mission were offered the loan of horses to ride. The man who provided them said that he had a nice quiet one 'for the little sister'. He was correct. We rode them quite often, during which time I realised that my horse needed encouragement to walk at all, let alone canter. However, on one occasion something mysterious occurred. At the top of the hill, overlooking the Dam, my horse suddenly took off and galloped down the hill. It took all my strength to hold on. The wall of the building housing the water pumping equipment loomed before my fearful eyes and I prayed one of those 'Sky Telegram Prayers' for help to avoid being thrown into the wall headfirst. The horse immediately put his two front legs firmly down onto the uneven ground and stopped. Somehow, I remained on the horse's back, shaken but in one piece. After that experience, the horse and I agreed to end the friendship!

Here we go again!

Christmas 1965. I noted in my diary: *The Christmas spirit is upon us once again! We are into carol singing and drama rehearsals, gift making and wrapping, making ward decorations*

Zulu style. Everyone appears to be loving the atmosphere working together as a team outside of their normal duty rota hours. Now I can say that I am looking forward to 1966 with hope and joy, enabling me to grow in the knowledge that my contribution is making a difference to the work and Christian ethos of this very special place.

CHAPTER SIX

A Learning Process!

M y midwifery knowledge in the UK had been learned from the standard textbook of midwifery written by Margaret Myles, or Maggie, as she was affectionately known. She was a hugely respected professional and renowned beyond the shores of Britain.

It was natural for me to continue to teach from this textbook and it served us well, but over time I encountered situations which were often only referred to in Margaret's book, and which I had not experienced before to coming to the Charley J. For example, mothers would sometimes have fits due to very high blood pressure (eclampsia).

This was a commonplace occurrence in this part of the world but was also extremely well managed with the use of a drug called Magnesium Sulphate. I do not recall our losing a single mother or her baby as a result of this. As noted earlier, I had learned that the shape of the Zulu women's pelves was different from those of European women. Zulu pelves tended to be predominantly the same shape as those of males, that is, pointed at the front, wider at the back. This meant that the foetal head could not fit (engage) into the front of the mother's pelvis prior to advanced (2nd stage onset) labour, at which point the baby's head would quickly rotate, descend and deliver immediately.

This was a good outcome but could have an element of shock for the baby and the risk of haemorrhage to the mother following the rapid delivery. However, the greater problem was if the foetal head did not rotate and descend. In this situation we had to carry out an emergency caesarean section to save the baby's life.

Another daily awareness was the need for careful 'history taking', an extremely important aspect of all medical, midwifery and obstetric work in order to avoid misdiagnosis. Obtaining accurate histories from our mothers was often difficult as they weren't too sure about the trustworthiness of the white people's medicine - a battle that Drs Anthony and Margaret had had to fight over the thirty-plus years of their medical work in that area.

An example of this was when one of our tiny premature babies died after much care, love, and the treatment of a chest infection. The mother then astounded us by thanking us in an attitude that was accepting of the whole situation, as though she was not surprised. On gentle questioning, she informed us that all the firstborn babies in her generational family had died following what appeared to be normal deliveries.

What had led to our ignorance of this really vital piece of information? The bereaved mother was immediately invited to return to the clinic for investigations and possible correction of the underlying cause, which we hoped would ensure a happier outcome in her next pregnancy.

There were further examples of 'cultural' surprises! One morning I was alerted to the fact that a waiting mother has absconded, as they so often did, I discovered! We were concerned because she was not in a good state of health. She returned later in the day and, in answer to my query, looked at me in amusement that I should need to ask. Her response to my query was, "I only went home to do my hair"!

The traditional Zulu hairstyle is a mixture of mud and hair styled into a plate like structure and allowed to harden, then embroidered with brightly coloured beads. The women sleep with a wooden support under their neck to preserve the hardened plate. They place a doughnut-shaped ring on top of their heads to carry sticks or buckets of water.

As they walk, their brightly coloured, delicate material scarves flow gracefully from their shoulders and they look beautiful. This woman was wanting to look her best for her forthcoming birth event! This added to my learning curve in understanding Zulu pregnancy and birth traditions.

A call for an ambulance at 7.30 one morning was to go to Nondweni, to be met at the local store by a man on horseback. He led us to an historical site, the Prince Imperial Monument, and then a further four or five miles to what we saw as an impassable ditch (known as a donga by Zulus). From there we walked up a steep hill carrying our equipment to the Kraal, and the hut where the mother was needing assistance. She had already given birth normally but the baby was small and premature. The placenta was lying nearby in a pool of blood.

Our Zulu midwife requested that all the female attendants leave the hut whilst we cleaned the mother and baby and made an assessment of the situation. It appeared that the lead 'attendant', which was usually the first wife, had cut the baby's umbilical cord level with the baby's flesh so we were not able to put on the usual ligature. Amazingly there was no visible bleeding and we wondered how she had prevented this? It would probably have been some sort of witchdoctor potion, a medicine or 'muthi' that would have been obtained at considerable cost prior to the expected birth. We were not, however, given the 'secret' of the medicine that had been applied to the cord wound.

The mother and baby needed to be admitted to hospital, so we said our farewells and started our return journey back to the hospital, but with a diversion to pick up an elderly lady who was unable to walk and needed treatment. When we eventually returned to the Charlie J Hospital later that day, with mother, baby, and the elderly lady, they were quickly settled into their respective ward beds and given the treatments needed to prevent infection. So in the end, all was well.

However, before we had time to retire to our beds two Norwegian doctors turned up from our sister Mission, Ekombe, about 30 miles away, bringing one of their patients who urgently needed a caesarean section. Her labour was obstructed to the point where her uterus was showing visible signs of impending rupture, described as a Bandles Ring in Margaret Myles textbook, but which I had never seen until now.

It was an alarming sight and obvious that the situation had to be dealt with urgently or both mother and baby would lose their lives. Thankfully, it was a situation that Dr Anthony Barker was familiar with and he was available to carry out the necessary caesarean procedure. We gave thanks and praise to God for His grace, mercy, timing and blessing. The Norwegian doctors did not possess the surgical skills to deal with the problem but had sought help immediately when the woman arrived on their hospital doorstep. This proved to be a pivotal decision in saving the mother and baby's life. They left us with joyful and grateful hearts knowing that they had done the right thing.

One day a student midwife urgently called for help, rushing to a car filled with Zulu women. One woman was in great distress, her undelivered baby's umbilical cord was visible between her legs, having prolapsed from the mother's womb, through a space between the pelvis and the baby's head. This was an extreme emergency as the baby would not be able to obtain oxygen from the cord if it was compressed completely. Regrettably there was no pulsation found in the cord and no heartbeat heard in the baby, so the mother was helped to deliver normally (rather than by caesarean section), though sadly knowing that her baby had died.

It was tragic but a wise decision as it soon became clear that the baby had been dead for some time. Doing an emergency caesarean section would have spread infection from the dead foetus, the mother would have suffered unnecessary surgery and we would have had a dilemma because our only surgeon, Dr Anthony Barker, was out at our furthest clinic, Manxili, where no telephone or radio contact was possible. Only a medical student was available at the hospital, and only capable of overseeing non-emergency situations.

One night at ten o'clock, we received a message to go to our nearest Anglican Mission station, St Augustine. On arrival we were directed to a local Kraal and a large hut which was well lit by candles, clean and welcoming. The labouring mother was in distress as her labour did not appear to be progressing and she was very tired.

An examination by our Zulu midwife revealed that the head of the baby was not descending into the mother's pelvis as we would hope in response to the mother's contractions. We needed to bring her back with us to the Charlie J Hospital for further assessment with the possibility of her needing an emergency caesarean section to deliver her baby safely. We carried her on a stretcher to the hospital truck and slowly travelled the extremely bumpy dirt track to our destination, an uncomfortable and painful journey for the mother.

On arrival, further examination showed a positive development! The bumps of the road had shifted the head of the baby into the correct position for entering the mother's pelvis enabling it to move down, rotate and deliver normally. In due course, an 8lb baby was born (6lb is the average weight of babies in this area) in good health.

This was a huge relief and delight to all following a very long night, but also another learning curve, that rough and bumpy tracks can be a blessing as well as a problem. However, I doubt this will ever feature as a prescribed method of treatment in the textbooks of the future!

A less positive aspect of traditional Zulu practice.

One morning I was distressed to find a mother is in the isolation area of the maternity unit because of infection caused by Zulu traditional midwives. They had cut the mother's labia with a piece of broken bottle to increase the space for the baby to be delivered (a primitive form of episiotomy).

Another pregnant mother was in a seriously dehydrated state resulting from an enema of magnesium prescribed by the local witchdoctor to get rid of an evil spirit. These were traditional harmful practices which I encountered for the first time. Whereas we could usually rescue the situation we wondered how these practices could be changed. An on-going challenge over time we suspected.

Extended midwifery practice.

Ever since my arrival, I had been encouraged by Maggie Barker to extend my range of midwifery skills in order to free up some of the doctors' time. This would mean that they could focus on the aspects of clinical practice which only they were qualified to do.

One such skill I acquired was suturing episiotomies, (these make more space so that the head of the baby can be delivered normally in the male-shaped narrow pelvic outlet.) I also learned to set up intravenous infusions (drips) when required for emergency fluid loss replacement and prior to caesarean section.

There was a high percentage of twin pregnancies in the area, at least four sets per month. In the UK, midwives would simply assist the obstetrician to deliver twins because of the greater risk of unexpected problems for mother and baby, and particularly for the second twin, whose head needs to enter the mother's pelvis in a short time in order to be delivered as normal.

Here I discovered that this role had been given to experienced midwives such as Sister Monica Mncube as an extension of their skills. I was now expected to pick up this role and to teach it to the student midwives. Thankfully, Dr Maggie

Barker and the Zulu qualified midwives were able to teach and guide me through each such situation until my skills and self-confidence had reached the necessary standard.

The same was expected for the management and delivery of babies with breech presentation - bottom first. My textbook knowledge of these was rapidly brought into practical outworking! Fear and anxiety at having to take this on was a real challenge as I knew the risks associated with such deliveries, but Maggie had taught the Zulu midwives extremely well and they worked with such calm confidence that they inspired me to do the same. The important lesson I learned was always to be prepared to ask for help whenever it was needed. Teamwork was essential to keep everyone safe.

These procedures would have been beyond the remit of my British qualification but the South African Nursing Council (whom I came to greatly respect in later years), showed wisdom and flexibility in allowing the development of Extended Nursing and Midwifery practice, but within their professional boundaries. This was key to saving lives when there were insufficient numbers of doctors, nurses and midwives to meet the growing demands on the Health Service.

When Dr Jon Larsen arrived, he taught me other practical skills such as how to use the ventouse (vacuum extraction) equipment which I had witnessed many times in the capable hands of Maggie Barker, but I needed to learn myself if the doctors were to extend their time in other capacities.

Forceps were rarely used, particularly the Keilland ones which only the brave, wise and really experienced obstetricians considered when faced with the situation where the baby's head had entered the mothers pelvic brim but had become stuck at a high level. This meant making a decision, whether to do a caesarean section or assist the birth manually, via the mother's vagina, pushing the baby's head up and applying the forceps to deliver the baby as normal. The latter was sometimes the wisest decision. If the woman lived in a remote Zulu area it could be likely that her people distrusted the white people's medical practices and she might not return to the hospital for delivery. If so, there was the risk that a previous caesarean section scar could rupture during future pregnancies. It was a rarely needed decision, and thankfully one which I was never asked to make! The ventouse was an amazingly effective and safe instrument to use as an alternative.

Zulu mothers had a strong instinct to suffer the pains of labour with their baby – 'otherwise Sister, I will not be able to love my baby'. For this reason they would not agree to an elective Caesarean Section unless they were allowed to be in labour for one hour! This was a revelation to me at that time but was confirmed repeatedly over the years in both Zulu and British midwifery practice. I came to realise that there was much that we could learn from mothers throughout the world about inbuilt instincts. We in our Western culture tend to have suppressed these in favour of modern approaches to childbearing, where pain is not to be tolerated and where breastfeeding is devalued.

The experiences outlined above have helped challenge my thinking, to explore other midwifery cultures , 'think outside the box', and learn from them. The prayer, Lord, grant me the wisdom, time and love to learn from my midwifery experience has proved beneficial!

CHAPTER SEVEN

The Importance of Friends

During the three-year period of my time at the Charley J Hospital I have had the privilege of working alongside and socialising with many lovely people from many different countries.

We have shared precious times of laughter, sadness, stories of frustration and anger. A lot of this resembled aspects of a large and continually changing family, held together by respect, love and an acknowledgment of each person's value and worth in contributing to the entire mission work.

The leadership skills of Drs Anthony and Maggie Barker were inspirational, encouraging and setting the highest standards in all aspects of the mission vision they had originally received. Like any family, we had our disagreements but we could voice our opinions, be heard, and trust our leaders to pray and reflect on what they had received. They would then give their decision based on their many years of experience living with the Zulu community, speaking their language fluently, seeking the opinions of the Zulu tribal leaders whenever that was required, and thereby gaining mutual respect even if they disagreed on some matters! It was difficult to know about such things in the short periods of time that some of us had signed up for.

There were other people who had a lasting and special place in our lives as we related together in the shared work and family life for a longer period. Married couples, with or without children, were wonderful in opening their hearts and homes to those of us who were single members of the mission community. We rarely felt lonely, excluded or rejected. For example, it was a joy and delight to be part of planning a wedding, perhaps by being a bridesmaid or making the dresses, making and icing the cakes, decorating the church altar rail with masses of pink and white wild Cosmos flowers - and this deepened relationships.

Invitations to baby sit, play with the little ones, read stories and take them for walks were most satisfying to those who, like me, hoped for a similar role in the future! - if it was in God's will and purpose.

A person of major influence on my life was Pamela Mead. The Matron of the Mission when I arrived in 1964, Pamela was a tall, largely-built woman, who welcomed me warmly and, at a later stage, invited me to share a large house with her. This solved one of the Mission's accommodation problems at that time and proved to be a positive move for all.

Pamela told me an amazing story of her entry into the world. She was one of twins but her mother went into premature labour and delivered her stillborn twin three months before Pamela was born. She was evidently very tiny (2 lbs) but survived to become the tall, large and extremely capable nurse that I knew and respected.

Pamela and I remained good friends for many years. After her retirement from the mission, she was accepted into an Anglican Nursing Order in Birmingham where we met up on frequent occasions, on my return to the U.K.

Our 'household' was further expanded in an unusual way. Following a weekend away from the Charlie J. we returned to the house to find a kitten curled up on a chair in the sitting room. We did not own a cat and had no idea who owned this one. On enquiring we drew a blank, no one on the mission or outside of it claimed the kitten, even though someone had spent money on having the necessary surgery to prevent further kittens.

Domino, as I called her due to her black and white markings, became part of our household and was quite a character. She remained with us at the Charley J until my contract was completed and I moved to another Mission Hospital near the Mozambique border, but that is another story. Domino lived to a ripe old age but sadly had to be put to sleep when a rabid dog got into the grounds of the mission and bit one of the domestic animals.

Another couple who became good friends were Jon and Jackie Larsen. They arrived in February 1965 and immediately Jon was put to work in his professional role as obstetrician/gynaecologist. Jackie helped out in various ways such as assistant to Phyllis Newton, the midwifery tutor at that time, and later took on the work of Dr Newton when he became ill. Dr Newton was the microbiologist who identified the numerous parasites which infested many of the patients. Jackie was pleased to be released from this rather smelly work when Dr Newton returned to work!

Working with Jon was a great pleasure. His professional knowledge, attitude and commitment to the task in hand, confirmed that this doctor knew exactly what he was doing, and that gave an unspoken sense of professional safety. He also came across as a man of integrity, humility and with a real love and respectful compassion for the Zulu people. He spoke fluent Zulu, having been brought up in the Natal area, so this was an immense advantage in building good relationships locally. Jon and Jackie, with their three children, Simon, Cathryn and David, became very good friends as we shared times together.

The Revd Peter and Mrs Bridget Burtwell are also included in this part of my Memory Lane! Bridget was a London Hospital trained nurse and gave her highly professional standards of care to the Mission for a number of years. We benefitted greatly from not only her nursing skills, but also from her social and personality qualities, bringing both laughter and challenge, and building up good relationships between us all.

Bridget has recently, sent me this note: "I think I started work at the Charley J in early 1996. We had visited before as we knew Jon Larsen of old as he had boarded with us in Cape Town. Anyway, one visit to the mission was enough to convince me that this was where I wanted to come and work. One afternoon, I rolled up in Nqutu in my specially purchased VW Beetle.

That was the beginning of an incredible few years. Everyone was so welcoming, including Biggie (an older generation lady) who was always trotting off to walk the Barkers' dog, to talk to the local magistrate or to run errands for Pete the Post to get extra cash "for her men". i.e. the patients under her care! The combination of Biggie and friend Lillian, plus we younger generation made us quite a gang! Peter used to arrive in his Toyopet to take services at the mission and, of course, to have coffee in the staff house afterwards. We really only got together seriously when he returned from furlough in the UK. We got married in February 1968 before the Barkers took an overseas holiday."

Another couple were Tony and Fiona Reynoldson. Tony arrived (alone) at the Charlie J in 1996, probably a little unprepared for what he would encounter with the engineering work that he was expected to manage. The previous engineer had left about three months earlier and Anthony Barker had realised that he had to find a temporary engineer to lead a team of approximately 30 men. Anthony knew that these men were lacking in team confidence and leadership and therefore would be unreliable in the work expected of them.

Anthony had met and recruited - from a high society wedding in South Africa - a handsome Scottish engineer to fill the gap until Tony arrived. It must have been quite a difficult period for the men though I didn't hear of any problems at the time. However, within a very short time of Tony's arrival, the men were heard singing together as a team, a sign that they were settling down under his leadership. They realised that here was a man who obviously knew what he was doing! I understand from Tony that it didn't stop them challenging him quite strongly at times but Tony was not fazed by this and gradually all was well and work progressed.

By now we all knew that Tony was engaged to be married and that Fiona would be joining him as soon as she could. She was only 19 years old and didn't know anyone else in South Africa except Tony. I knew what that felt like so was immediately willing to help in whatever way was necessary.

Fiona wanted to have three bridesmaids so Bridget Burtwell, Sally Strang and myself offered our services. We made our dresses out of a lovely blue shiny material. All of us had basic skills in dressmaking but Sally was probably more skilled than Bridget or me. We shared many a laugh completing this joyful project and we hoped that Fiona was pleased with the results. She certainly looked a very beautiful bride on the day and all those who could shared in the celebration party after a traditional marriage service in the hospital chapel of Christ the King. The chapel looked wonderful, with pink, white and red Cosmos flowers gathered from the countryside verges and piled up in front of the altar area.

The celebration following the service was very much in Zulu style. The women, singing and dancing, swept the ground with palm leaves in front of the bride and groom to get rid of any evil spirits and bring good ones. The large, gathering of people sharing a food feast, speeches, singing, more dancing and processions made for a very emotional and uniting time of British and Zulu cultures.

Another friend, Dorothy Maclean, was one of the visitors to our hospital who caught my attention. Dorothy loved the Zulu people and coined the phrase 'Black is Beautiful'. It was her encouragement to them to embrace their colour and be proud of it. This helped them to have a positive sense of self-worth. Dorothy was a talented pianist, also loved singing and appreciated the Zulu people's natural harmonising ability.

A gift God had given me was a good singing voice. It had been enjoyed and used with various choirs, school, and church events prior to coming to the mission, and Dorothy encouraged me to continue to use my voice alongside the other instrumental and singing traditions represented on the mission. Singing was seen as a part of daily life to express emotions of happiness and joy, as well as empathy for those suffering pain, hardship and 'Valley of Death' experiences.

Listening to Zulu people softly chanting Negro-type spirituals reminded us of where our help really came from. A student midwife named Dorcas taught us the song –

'Turn your eyes upon Jesus,
Look full on His wonderful face,
And the things of earth will grow strangely dim
In the Light of His Glory and Grace'

We used to sing this softly together when life was sad or difficult and it was always comforting to the spirit and emotions.

The end of my 3-year contract was now approaching, and I realised that it was time to reflect on the outcomes of these years in terms of the spiritual, emotional, professional and social aspects. I had increasingly come to love and respect the medical, nursing, midwifery, domestic and many other people who supported the work within the mission and also from outside, those of the Zulu community living in the district where we served. It was also time to begin to think of the next step in my future.

As my midwifery skills had developed I had been asked to consider being a Midwifery Examiner for King Edward VIII Hospital midwifery students in Durban, my role being to carry out the Oral part of the state examination. This was the largest hospital in South Africa for black women needing obstetric care, so it had been with some nervousness that I had agreed to broaden my professional boundaries by undertaking this task, particularly as I was not a qualified Midwifery Teacher and needed special permission by the South African Nursing Council to be able to agree to take this on (which they did!).

I had found that my working colleagues there were just as friendly and accepting as those in our, and other, hospitals; reciprocal arrangements brought a sharing of relational aspects beneficial to all.

During these visits, I was given a unique opportunity to see the management care of their preterm babies. The annual total of deliveries at this hospital was enormous and the preterm statistics very high. The demand for incubators and other supporting care needs (including trained assistants/midwives) was beyond the hospital's ability to provide. The hospital recognised that an alternative strategy was required if the infant mortality rate was to be reduced. The management decided to encourage the mothers to provide their human body warmth and link emotional basic needs to their own babies by placing the baby between their breasts. This linked the 'in-womb relationship' with the mother to the post-delivery relationship, the 'bonding' which is crucial for the human needs of a sense of being and self-worth, significance and security if we are to thrive.

This is well known by midwives and mothers to be particularly important in the first twenty-four hours of life, when mothers and babies instinctively want to be together. Separation at this point gives rise to severe anxiety in both, though in emergency situations may be necessary. Hearing the mother's familiar heartbeat and voice gives reassurance to the baby, especially if severely premature.

As at the Charley J the mothers were taught to feed their own babies with expressed breast milk by teaspoon, glass pipettes or tube until the baby was well and strong enough to feed at the breast. I had seen that this regime worked well for mothers and babies, the only drawback being that it required quite a long period in hospital, giving rise to some family difficulties if the extended family were not in place to help out.

We had been impressed with the outcome of the Durban hospital's care management and had brought their principles into our little unit. We saw that our babies were thriving in similar manner, and were catching up with the 'target' milestones on the now universally accepted 'Centile Graph Charts'

We were in a possibly unique position of being able to regularly check our babies at our local and outer geographical clinics for five years, or even longer. There was great opportunity to see a child's progress within the family setting, an opportunity which I reflected was not at that time in place in the NHS at home.

And so to the big question. Should I consider renewing my contract with U.S.P.G. for a further 3 years?

The one aspect of my time at the Charley J which had caused some degree of spiritual distress was that I could see something in my missionary colleagues which was beautiful, desirable and attractive to all with whom they came into contact. But I felt strongly and sadly that that 'something' was missing in me!

As a result of much reflection and agonising I felt that the honest decision would be not to continue at the Charley J, or indeed anywhere else, as a missionary. I came to the conclusion that it would be more honest to look for a role in another hospital in the UK, solely on a professional basis as Nurse/Midwife rather than a spiritual one.

This decision met with some resistance and sadness from Drs Anthony and Maggie Barker and others on the mission, but they respected it and as the last six weeks approached there were harrowing farewells as arrangements for my departure began to take place.

However, things then took a rather unexpected turn...

CHAPTER EIGHT

An Unexpected Change of Direction

Having made the difficult and painful decision that I should return at the end of my contract to the UK and look for a 'secular' hospital job there, I resolved to finish my time at the Charley J fulfilling an established missionary aim, to 'finish well'. However, as already mentioned, things took a rather unexpected turn...

From the time of my arrival there were a few gentlemen who caused my heart to skip a beat, such as the delightful Alistair in his kilt, the afore-mentioned Scottish engineer, kind and thoughtful to everyone but who simply 'tolerated' the obvious affections of this new young missionary.

There were also a number of medical students and newly-qualified doctors from both Britain and America, such as David Fielding with his beautiful musical ability and sensitive, thoughtful character. And Eli Dayton, a uniquely interesting person. Both of these captured my attentions (but not necessarily theirs!) for a while, and left holes of sadness when they left the Charlie J.

Nevertheless, the experiences gave me a confidence that I might be presentable as a marriage partner one day. I was not alone in assessing the romantic stakes in this large mission community in the remote area of Nqutu Zululand; romances were part of life and added spice to it. Some did get married on the mission, inviting all of us to share in their joy and happiness for the day, and some remained friends for many years afterwards.

On returning to my thatched mud hut after a duty shift one day, it was to find my bed covered with red roses! Where did these come from? Forty miles from the nearest small town, had someone been there? And was there even a florist there? Who could have sent them?

On enquiring of various sources I was told that the roses were from our most recent employee from Durban, the new hospital administrator. He and I had only a superficial social acquaintance at this time so it was a romantic gesture, exciting, but a little discomforting and unsettling in the period set aside for the preparations for leaving.

We met and had the necessary conversations about this unexpected situation, and we agreed that we would spend as much time as we could in the remaining weeks to consider what might be the outcome of this relationship. It was a pleasant but uneasy time for me, a time for much prayer and agonising. At the end of this period I came to the decision that it was too early in the relationship to accept a proposal of marriage and I asked that he would agree to 'friendship communications' and wait to see how the relationship would develop.

My would-be suitor was not happy with this suggestion and applied emotional pressure as earnestly as he could, but I held to my decision and made it onto the departure plane armed with a large teddy bear and promises of courtship at a distance for the foreseeable future!

What next?

During the next year he was faithful to his promise, many love letters, small gifts and telephone calls were received and reciprocated, and the time came when I felt that I was ready to accept another proposal of marriage. His delight was evident, and a diamond engagement ring soon arrived. And finally, a date was set for me to return to Durban, South Africa, to marry.

Meanwhile, I had been accepted, and returned to, Gloucester Hospital as a Nurse whilst also completing the various commitments of deputation talks throughout the U.S.P.G. Anglican Church programme, enhanced by a preselected set of slides of my involvement with the CJMH Mission.

Making my personal news known to my family, friends and nursing colleagues and management employers was difficult. They were sad at losing me to another country but also shared in the prospect of marital joy for me in the future. Wedding gifts arrived from so many lovely friends and family, thoroughly overwhelming at times. The prospect of saying goodbye to my family had an element of heartbreak about it as my future husband and I would not have the financial means to travel between our two countries when we might want to.

Departure day came yet again, on the 3rd January 1969, on board the S.A.Oranje from Southampton to Cape Town, once again accompanied by many sadnesses, yet this time I was returning to the South Africa that, in spite of the apartheid regime, I had grown to love. And I was returning to meet the fiancé I had not seen for eighteen long and busy months. As the plane circled around Durban airport I became aware that my excitement was tinged with a degree of nervousness, a nervousness that increased as we prepared to land.

As I emerged from the plane, I scanned the faces of the crowd waiting to meet the plane, and there he was, armed with a huge bouquet of flowers including the wonderful South African Proteas. Dear, faithful man, looking so happy. And yet, as I stood at the top of the plane steps and look down into his upturned face, I felt a terrible chill of unknowing. Had I made a huge mistake? Had my love for him been built on an imaginary 'virtual' relationship and not on reality? I suddenly felt sick at heart, bewildered, lost. In those few moments at the top of the aeroplane's steps I became very certain that I had made a truly terrible mistake. I knew now that I really couldn't go through with the intended marriage.

Should this dear man be told now, or should I wait for confirmation of these terrible feelings over the weekend? The plan was to meet up with his mother and the three of us to spend time getting to know each other. But I knew that I could not enter into a relationship, of continuing deception, now that I believed that my true feelings had been revealed. And so on the way to the hotel I told him what I now knew to be the truth.

He was understandably devastated by the news, indeed could not really accept it. The planned weekend was one of the most difficult and painful of my younger years. Both he and his mother spent the weekend trying to persuade me to change my mind. It was very difficult to resist, as I had no money to return home, no job, no family to turn to for help. For my now former fiancé it was equally difficult. He now found himself in the position of having no wife-to-be, no job in the Mission Hospital where we had met, and the possibility of being unable to take up a very good working position in the USA, which he had been offered and had accepted assuming that he would be married.

I was distressed, confused, felt very much alone. Where was God in this situation? And why had He brought me back to this troubled country? Nothing made sense.

As the allotted days there passed and my situation became more stable I began to wonder whether I had been brought back to

Africa for another purpose. I resolved that I needed to be very sure of finding His guidance for the next part of my life journey. In my distress, I contacted Drs Anthony and Maggie Barker and told them about my plight. I asked that I might return to the Charley J to work, in return for board and lodging until I had secured another nursing post elsewhere. With typical love and generosity, they welcomed me back and agreed to allow to stay until such time as the Lord would make His will and purpose clear. Thus ended a very sad chapter in my life.

CHAPTER 9

Moving On

It was with a degree of shame and embarrassment as well as thankfulness and joy, that I returned to the Charley J, but the loving welcome from the Barkers, nursing and midwifery colleagues settled me down to serve in whatever capacity was required.

This involved more midwifery teaching in the classroom and at the bedside, theatre and neonatal unit. I also took on 'Super Midwife' roles and travelled to other mission hospitals, including another visit to the King Edward VIII Hospital in Durban, 350 kilometres away, as Oral examiner for the South African Midwifery Council. At the King Edward VIII Hospital my knowledge, respect and admiration increased as I witnessed again their response to the overwhelming challenge of caring for huge numbers of premature babies with insufficient staff and equipment.

Meeting up with past friends.

During this unexpected extra time at the hospital, I was blessed to welcome Drs Robert and Celia Brown and their two young children, Dee Dee and Tony. This was a hugely emotional event for me as Celia Brown had been a working colleague at the

Gloucester City Hospital (Gynaecological M1 Ward) where I was and we had become friends.

When Celia had days off and needed some non-medical company, she had come to my home where I lived with my mother, a small semi-detached two-bedroom house with open coal fires and without modern luxuries. She had slotted in like one of the family, and we had enjoyed each other's company. When she had given me her news of meeting Drs Anthony and Margaret Barker and had told me of her 'Yes' response to their invitation of working at the Mission with them, I had been excited for her, but selfishly sad at the prospect of not seeing her again.

We had agreed to keep in touch by letter, and some years later Celia had suggested that I come to join her at the Charles Johnson Memorial Hospital at Nqutu in KwaZulu - Natal. That had seemed to me to be to be a good plan of action, as it would be a good place to obtain the practical experience required prior to working in Kenya, the country of my original vision. I had been advised by the United Society of the Propagation of the Gospel (U.S. P. G.) to first do some missionary training and completed the required 6 months at the College of Ascension, an Anglican Convent in Birmingham.

However, by the time that I arrived at the Charley J, Celia had met Robert Brown, a medical student who had chosen to do his elective period of experience at the Mission. They fell in love with each other and at an appropriate date, moved to America where they married.

Now they had returned to the Charley J (as Celia had said they would) to work again. What a joyful renewal of friendship between Celia and myself. How good also to meet Robert, who was most gracious in his acceptance of me as a friend of his wife, and to meet their little ones. We spent as much social time together as our daily working lives would allow, to enable 'a getting to know you' and 'catching up on' events which had taken place in the period we had been apart. A precious time.

I believe it was later in this year that Dr Anthony asked me to bake a birthday cake for Celia's mother. "Of course I will," I responded. "When will she be visiting?"

Anthony, with great surprise said: "Jules - don't you know about Celia and her brother? Lady Audrey Fiennes is their mother and she is already here with us. I will introduce you to her today!

How ignorant and stupid, I felt, and even somewhat intimidated. I was not at all comfortable with this newly acquired knowledge, and wondered if this would get in the way of my friendship with Celia. I need not have worried - both Celia and her mother proved to be loving, warm-hearted friends. And when eventually we had all left the Charley J we kept in touch from time to time right up until their deaths years later. Lady Fiennes sent me a Christmas card for some years reminding me of the birthday cake and signing herself as 'Celia's mother'.

New developments.

During the time I was away in the UK, an Old People's Home had been completed. This was in response to the forced relocation of 'township Black people' to the area, with no supporting infrastructure or family support for elderly folk who needed shelter and care.

The building was a circular shape, thatched and surrounded by a central grassed area where the residents could sit in sun or shade, protected from the wind. It was empty at this time, awaiting a couple, Peter and Felicity Eliastam, who had accepted the challenge of being the wardens of the new venture. I was totally unprepared for the "whirlwind personality" of Peter. His beautiful wife Felicity was of a calmer nature but their interaction with each other was inspiring!

Peter came from an orthodox Jewish background and taught me what this meant and the radical changes that had come about when he had accepted Jesus as his Messiah (referring to this state as that of a 'Completed' or 'Messianic Jew'). His zeal for his Lord was passionate. He demonstrated this through art with wonderful collages and paintings. His passion was also wonderfully expressed in his evangelistic teaching. He and Felicity had paid the usual price of Peter's conversion to Christianity - rejection by his orthodox Jewish family including any expected future inheritance, a great sadness for this lovely couple. Their amazing new Christian journey had truly involved a period of 'living by faith'.

Later in the year I shared in the honour of delivering their baby daughter, Maria, and was able to enjoy their company until I left the hospital later in 1969. My awareness of the historical roots of Jesus grew steadily from that time, giving me a love of the Old Testament, which has never left me.

Felicity's strong faith was sorely tested when they returned to Johannesburg on completion of their contract at the Charlie J and she became seriously ill. I was contacted urgently and asked to go and pray with them as a family, to ask the Lord to save her life. This I did and found Felicity unable to move out of bed, with hugely swollen legs and body, suffering greatly. Peter and Felicity's children were still very young and they were naturally very anxious for the future without her. We all prayed, including little Maria who, only a short time before, had asked the Lord into her life and had prayed in tongues!

Felicity's faith remained strong, and some months later they contacted me with wonderful news of a miraculous healing. Felicity and family had taken a holiday by the sea and she was not only able to move but was running along the beach completely free from the disease which had threatened to take her life.

Another life changing relationship which impacted my life that year was that of meeting the Rev Dr Clifford Allwood and his lovely wife Anne.

Clifford had requested to come to the Charlie J to learn how to perform a caesarean section under local anaesthetic. Anthony

Barker had perfected the technique over the years due to the unavailability of anaesthetists and/or anaesthetic gases at the Mission. As an ordained Methodist minister, holding an agricultural degree, Clifford had studied medicine with the support of the Methodist church and was now responding to their request to go to Manguzi mission in Maputa, Kwa Zulu, Natal, and build up the surgical facilities there, with a specific focus on saving the lives of childbearing women who were dying in childbirth due to obstructed labour with no access to emergency Caesarian Section. The existing clinic/hospital did not provide this facility but needed to do so as soon as possible as there were 33,000 people in the area, many of whom suffered from a specific Maputo hip disease, which compromised their ability to deliver their babies normally.

Clifford spoke fluent Zulu and was welcomed by the Charley J community with ease and enthusiasm. He was a joy to work with, spiritually encouraging and socially engaging. Anne was equally engaging in different and positive ways, supportive of God's calling on their lives and open to learning how God was going to use their skills and gifts in this new, scary phase of their married life. We quickly became friends and as the year progressed, I felt an urge to ask Clifford if he 'could use a Midwife/Nurse' in the planned project next year!

He gladly accepted my offer, much to my relief (that I had further employment,) but also because of the nature of the experience that could be useful to both of us in the future.

And so it was that the season of life at the beloved Charles Johnson Memorial Hospital came to an end with thankfulness and gratitude for all the positive experiences which helped me to grow into a healthier, more mature person, able to reach out to others who need encouragement along the way.

It was also the beginning of the next phase of the journey with a God who was teaching me so much about His personal love for me.

And finally, to answer a question!
What about the original vision?

My vision came to me as an eight-year-old reading Albert Schweitzer's book about his work as a Christian doctor in Africa, and his work happened to be in a hospital in Kenya. Over the years I hung on to that vision and took steps to fulfil it, but those steps simply took me to a different part of that great country, Africa. And so I believe that God's original vision was indeed for me to be a Nursing Missionary in Africa – but not Kenya-, for me it was in South Africa. Sometimes we get the minor details wrong!

And certainly over all those years our loving Lord sustained, guided, taught and encouraged me throughout His outworking of the vision, and I give thanks and praise that what the Lord calls us to, in service and ministry, He brings to completion according to His will and purpose.

Earth's crammed
      with Heaven
& every common bush
      afire with GOD.
But
only he who sees
takes off his shoes —
           E.B. Browning

With Christmas wishes
from Maggie & Anthony
           Barker

14a Lansdowne Road, Wimbledon.

Short Stories

A Watery End

Returning from a weekend away from a remotely situated Mission Hospital near the Mozambique Border of South Africa, 10 miles from the Indian Ocean and 80 miles from the Ubombo Mountain range and small town of Mkuze, my passenger Mrs. Lambourne and I, called in at our sister Hospital, Bethesda, set at the top of the mountain. This was to greet and renew brief fellowship with our mission colleagues but also to use the radio to contact our hospital and tell them we were on our way and would reach them in 2 hours time, all being well. This was our agreed custom, set up to give some protection for ourselves and visitors as we crossed the sand and bush scrub road towards the Indian Ocean and home. If we did not arrive in the time margin the Hospital would send a Land Rover out to find us.

On this occasion, our lovely Medical Superintendant Dr Clifford Allwood, informed us that, since we had been away, there had been torrential rain with the consequences of extensive flooding. He therefore set a new time limit of 4 hours!

We set off down the mud, rock and extremely steep mountain road. All well, negotiated safely, and onto the' flats of mud and sand roads towards Manguzi Hospital, home for 'Lambi' and me. Lambi (Mrs Lambourne) was an elderly but incredibly strong and practically skilled lady who ran the hospital laundry and catering departments with a rod of iron! However we did discover, from time to time, that she had a compassionate heart and would help anyone with a genuine need. She was also a character who suffered with her nerves and at the beginning of this journey was already in a state of agitation! As we drove through a short distance of forest and onto the scrubland towards the only road sign at a 'T' junction, it looked as if we would be alright, no water to be seen anywhere, what a relief! No sooner had I made this remark to my nervous passenger than the reality of the situation became clear! We found ourselves facing a vast expanse of water with only the local Palm fronds sticking out of it. We knew we had to make for the only road sign in the area and go to the right of it! We were driving my newly acquired VW Beetle, bought, on loan, for me by the S.A.Methodist Mission as a prerequisite for my taking up a contract with them. It was considered necessary for maintenance of our health to be able to get away from the sub-tropical and Malaria infested area on a regular basis. Having shared this information with some medical students at my previous mission, a snippet of what was said by one of them at the time, was that, providing all the seals were intact - and because the engine was in the back of the car and had a front wheel drive - the car was capable of floating! All one had to do was keep it in first gear until the grip of the road was felt! At the time I took all this with a 'large pinch of salt'! I remembered thinking 'What a tall story- how gullible does he think I am?'. But here we are in a situation which requires me to put it to the test if we are to make any progress at all. So, into first gear we go and 'chug' along towards the road sign, float towards the right of it and continued for several miles until we felt the wheels of the car grip the sand. 'Oh ye of little faith a voice was saying to me!' I gave a prayer of thanks for the student who had shared that seemingly useless piece of information over a lunchtime meal some time before this event. From the time of reaching more solid ground, I was able to get out of the car and stick pieces of palm tree into the solid bits of underwater road and negotiate the way forward. This we did for many of the 80 miles until we reached the outskirts of the Maputo village and saw the familiar, narrow, bridge which we had to cross. I had a fallen tree along its length but it looked as if the remaining width would be sufficient for us to pass over the short distance to the other side. Poor Lambi was, by now, in a desperate state of anxiety and for some time had been crying out 'we are going to die ', a comment which did not do a lot for me as driver! I made the decision to go onto the bridge and trust it to hold, which I did. On doing so we could see that the left-hand side of the bridge had been demolished! Thankfully the right-hand side held us till we reached the safety of the road. Here we were faced with an enormous 4-wheel based truck with a freezer attachment. These were quite often seen in our area. They were owned by individuals, or companies from Johannesburg who fished in the local National Game Park lakes for fish called Grunter which were large, full of flavour and much sought after - including the local people and us! From the great height of his cab, the Afrikaans driver called down to me 'What's the road like Missie?' I replied, 'Very bad - come with me to our mission, stay the night and then we will help escort you onto the road tomorrow.' He looked at us and laughed. I felt indignant at this response until, reflecting on it later, realised that to him we were two women, one in her twenties and one elderly, in a VW Beetle car who had come through the floods successfully. Who did we think we were kidding,?. It must have looked laughable to him. However he did not get far – he and his truck got stuck and had to be rescued by the local police until he could safely go on his way several days later. We did get home safely, four hours from our starting point, and received a warm welcome from our friends at the hospital. Twenty fours later both Lambi and I suffered from delayed shock / anxiety of the journey and needed two days rest to recover!

A few days after the floating car journey, a group of us went to see the damaged bridge and the extent of damage to the road following the floods. What we saw was an amazing scene of emerging beauty and new life in the midst of debris and damage to the village homes and crops. The area, which prior to flooding, had been pure sand (to a depth of 2000 Feet, according to an Oil Exploration Survey) was now transformed into a series of small lakes with waterlilies of every colour and crowded with wetland wildlife such as I had never seen before in that place. Spoonbills, large Egrets, Flamingo and Pelicans! In addition at nearby pools there was a local Zulu man using a handmade tricorn shaped hat, made of the local Palm, to fish. The small fish were jumping about in the hats as the water drained away - hundreds of brown sparkling creatures! Where had they come from? We received a suggestion that seeds of flowers and eggs of the fish, may have lain dormant in the sand for many years. Is that possible? Whatever the truth, it appeared to me to be a miracle. The Bible says, "How wonderful is our God who can bring forth life from the desert." and we witnessed for ourselves, the results of life coming forth from the desert.

Khozi Bay

A small group of us from our Manguzi Mission Hospital staff, black and white, (during the Apartheid years of the early 60's) went by Land Rover to the nearest lake for a time of rest and relaxation. The lakes originated from the Indian Ocean nearby, its waters running into successive ones, each one becoming less salty as the lakes were formed. Wonderful fish, such as Grunter, a delicious flavoured, white-fleshed fish much sought after in the area were found in the initial lake. The local people made and set basket traps, wide entrance and tapering to a small hole , within the entrance to the lake. The fish would be able to swim through but not return. It appeared to work well and was a very important protein source of nutrition for the Tongan/Zulu of the area. However they did have competition from the fishermen/ business people from Johannesburg who came with very large trucks to fish for them and sell them at inflated prices.

The lakes were separated from the sea by a beautiful wide beach and large, high sand dunes. The water in the lake system became increasingly dark as it reached the last lake. As a result it became a mirror reflecting the overhanging trees, sub-tropical jungle, and supported the wonderfully varied, blue, pink and white water lilies. Each of these lakes had residents of Hippopotami and Crocodiles. It was an area of outstanding beauty and under the protection of the National Parks Board. The protection also included that of Leatherback and Saddleback Turtles who returned to the beaches each year to lay their eggs – a sight I was privileged to see at a later date.

On this particular trip, the group settled down on the sandy beach around the lake, enjoyed a picnic together, singing and laughing on the hot but less humid environment of the lake. The children with us were allowed, under watchful parental eyes, to paddle and play on the edge of the shallow waters. Suddenly we heard a shout from the deeper water further out on the lake flats where our hospital administrator, Howard, had been swimming. It was unusual for any of the "resident lake animals" to come near the shallow flats between 10.00am and 4.00pm, but here was our friend being pursued by a large Hippo, who obviously objected to sharing his bath with a human being. We watched with a mixture of anxiety, amusement and shouting encouragement to Howard as he "ran on water" across the flats to the safety of the beach. We all gave a sigh of relief as we saw the Hippo return to the deeper waters where his fellow family were watching. We decided it would be a wise decision to stick to the unwritten rules of nature and not argue with the animals, whose home it had been for many years. This was not so easy for the Tongan/Zulu people who lived there and who depended on eking a living from fish trapping and growing crops. The Hippo came out at night to find food and would desecrate the area doing so. Any brave soul trying to chase them off would be in great danger of severe injury or death. Thankfully this did not happen very often, possibly because of a mutual respect of boundaries? Living with nature is one with risks in this particular area of South Africa, but worth it for its beauty and bounty.

The Moon Man

Coming off duty at the end of a routine hospital, outpatient day, and making my way up through the lovely green lawns. Citrus fruits heavy with their Lemon and Orange blossom fragrance, towards my little wooden chalet style home, I was startled to see the figure of a tall , white man , shaven headed and dressed in what seemed to be a gold and white space suit and pushing a motorbike! This was not a sight one usually saw in the sub-tropical, sandy and forested area of Maputa, KwaZulu, Natal which ran 5 miles parallel to the border of Mozambique with its capital Maputo.

It fell to me to welcome him to our hospital (visitors of this kind were rare, i.e. White people, without a Visa, during these Apartheid years).? He therefore needed to be given hospitality within the hospital boundaries and his name recorded in a Register by the local police command. I took him to our Visitor Accommodation, introduced him to the household who were enjoying their afternoon tea and made him feel as welcome as we could., whilst his motorbike underwent repairs by our hospital engineers who seemed to be able to mend anything!

He settled in quickly, turned out to be a friendly, and obviously well-travelled and confident man. He told us he was an author, researching material for his latest book. This necessitated a journey from Mozambique to South Africa which he decided to make by motorbike. All went well until his transport broke down (not surprising given the extremely sandy terrain he was crossing!)

He had followed a stony track towards a Border Town called Josini which was near to an American Mission Hospital. It occurred to us that he had probably got lost along the way, as the distance between the Mission and ourselves was between 60/80 miles and any other civilisation in our vicinity which, at that time in history, was not on any official map but which was home to 33,000 Zulu Tongan people who had not been registered as being born. . During his stay with us he demonstrated some rather flirtatious attitudes, he invited me to "wash his back like his maids did in Hong Kong"! This invitation I strictly turned down and made sure I was accompanied by a second person whenever needing to visit him for any purposes! However he was a 'fun person' to have around and brought some laughter and unexpected cheer into our long, unrelenting, work filled days for a brief period of time. We said farewell to him and off he went. Imagine my surprise when, some time later, a large parcel arrived for me. Inside, wrapped in many layers of tissue paper was a beautiful, quilted, Chinese, orange-coloured dressing gown, with a gold embossed letterhead note of thanks for hospitality! There was obviously some truth in what he had told us. How I wish that I might have read his book - if he ever wrote it - that is.

A Heart Stopping Time

One day, an invitation came, from a friend, to join them on a safari expedition, in the game reserve, at Hluhlue, Near the Umfolozi river. On the morning of departure, The group were instructed, by the senior white game ranger, that we would need to walk in single file, in silence, which he doubted we ladies could do, otherwise we might stand in danger of being attacked by animals. He added that if we were attacked, we would need to be prepared to shin up the nearest tree, even if it was one with large thorns, we laughed. He, however, was not amused and said that we would need to do it, if the need arose, then have to decide how we would get down. He directed that he would walk in front of us all, with his gun loaded, With a black ranger at the back of the group, with his gun also loaded. it was a truly beautiful day, not too hot, with the delicious fragrance of the acacia trees heavy on the light breeze. So, we set off. We were, by this time, very mindful of the need to be silent and alert. We really wanted to see the animals, so we were very desirous of the need to not startle them, but to recognise ourselves as merely visitors, temporarily in their territory. The animals ,we were told we were likely to see, were lion, zebra, wart hogs, giraffe and various kinds of antelope , or bok. Also, we stood a high chance of seeing a variety of birds, including fish eagle and vultures. We walked until mid-morning, when we approached a lake, Where we were told we might well encounter crocodile or hippo. We all sat on the perimeter of the lake, at a safe distance.

The white ranger told the black ranger to go and fetch water, from the lake, for our refreshment. On the way, the white ranger had teased the black ranger, on a number of occasions, that he might be attacked by something, so the poor man kept jumping into the air, with alarm. While the group was resting, I decided that this presented a good opportunity to answer a call of nature... having walked a few yards around an area of bush and scrub, I was very suddenly confronted by a large crocodile, basking in the morning sun. I remember wondering who was more surprised, as we both transfixed each other.

Who was going to blink first? I found that I could actually physically not move... this initial encounter was probably only a few seconds but felt like an eternity! It was only when the crocodile started, slowly, to get up on one of the front legs that this suspended moment was broken. However, even though my brain registered that he was beginning to be on the move, I somehow remained completely immobile. It was not until the crocodile had stood up, on all four legs, in front of me, that I realised just how enormous it was. When it moved one of its huge legs towards me, I was very suddenly galvanised into action, Turning around quickly and immediately running back to the group. As I ran, I could hear a resounding splash, which I hoped was the crocodile going into the lake. Amazingly, I had still not fulfilled the call of nature, which was my original purpose! As I approached the group, who were yet unaware of my absence, it was reassuring, to hear them laughing and joking and talking about what they had seen so far.

However, I realised that the white ranger would be very annoyed at my having gone off, without notifying them. as I was, now, somewhat more afraid of the Ranger than I had been of the crocodile, I sauntered back to join the group, as if I had simply been for a short Sunday afternoon stroll with an air of nonchalance. Soon after, the Ranger told us that we were now going to go around the area of Bush and scrubland to the left, saying that we needed to be particularly careful, as large crocodiles frequently basked in the morning sun, around there. The delicious irony of having just encountered one, at particularly close quarters, was not lost on me...

The Rangers and the rest of my travelling companions knew nothing of this at all...

I Am Found

One year following a move from the Charles Johnson Memorial Hospital Nqutu KwaZulu R.S.A. to another Mission, Manguzi Hospital, Maputa. KwaZulu, Natal, our only doctor, needed to have a well-earned rest. He had been given the task, by the Methodist Church of South Africa, to develop an existing small hospital/clinic into one where Caesarean Sections could be carried out. There was concern that pregnant mothers were dying because of complications in giving birth. It appeared that surgical intervention to help them was not always available and this needed to change. The existing hospital/clinic treated people with medical conditions, all the beds plus floor beds were mainly taken up with patients suffering from Tuberculosis The doctor and his wife who had headed up the medical work in the area for some years, were retiring and leaving the hospital which gave the opportunity for changes to be made.

Our doctor was well loved, well qualified with Degrees and life experience in Farming, Medicine and ordination as a Methodist Minister. He had responded to this 'call on his Christian life' with enthusiasm and efficiency by teaching me and another British white nurse how to run the hospital in his absence. My colleague, Jean, learned how to look after the newly opened 'bush clinics'. Literally, a Land Rover pulling up at a locally agreed place, under a tree, where the Zulu people would be waiting for medical attention. From the back of the Land Rover, Jean would undertake the tasks of weighing babies, checking people for signs of T.B. attending to wounds, pulling badly decayed teeth, and on rarer occasions, delivering a baby!

She responded enthusiastically to the task given to her and this resulted in a mutual building up of trusting relationships between the local people and ourselves at the hospital base. Quite often she would be accompanied by Dr Clifford Allwood and by a local Zulu man who was employed as Chaplain to the hospital. He later volunteered to walk each day, within a 5-mile radius, to follow up the discharged T.B. patients to check and encourage the lifesaving routine of taking their medication as prescribed. It also gave him the opportunity to evangelise and link the spiritual input to their lives with the reality of everyday practicalities which could be overwhelming due to the debilitating nature of their illness.

In the meantime, I was given the task to look after the 280 bedded hospital when Dr Allwood was not available! This required training in such additional things as Outpatients, performing minor surgery, prescribing appropriate medication and responding to unexpected emergencies brought to our door each day. This was in addition to Jean and myself teaching locally employed people to clean the wards, make beds, boil a set instruments to sterilise them for surgery preparation, assist patients to the toilet, wash newly admitted patients who generally were in a sad state of personal hygiene, (quite often very smelly! Having to fetch containers of water from a badly polluted river possibly many miles away was a contributing factor to this), and giving practical demonstrations on the Isolation procedures required when patients were admitted with serious infections such as Typhoid, Paratyphoid, Dysenteries etc. It was a slow and often frustrating process but eventually brought forth fruit!

The time came when Dr Allwood was ordered by the Mission Management to take a health break, away from the area, which was a Malaria black spot and one where most medically trained people would not apply to for jobs because of the death rate and high risks associated with it. Our loved doctor was tired and needed a rest.

The time had come to test how well Jean and myself had been prepared for such a moment as this.

All went well initially, the hospital was full but patients responding to their various treatments, the daily clinics, at the hospital and in the bush, continued as usual. Then we suffered a serious Cyclone which cut us off from any communication by telephone, road or any other route, with our other mission hospitals 40 - 80 miles away. At that time a mother had walked through a dreadful terrain of flood water, mud and fallen trees holding her lovely 3-month-old baby above her head to get help as he was very sick with a fever. I examined the little one and registered how ill the child was but also how much the mother looked to me as the 'White Nurse' to bring healing for her child.

This was an awesome responsibility which put me under considerable pressure, particularly as my diagnostic skills seemed to have deserted me at this crucial time. Admitting that I needed help but was unable to access it via the usual routes, I walked up to my little house trying to find a solution to the problem but also very angry with the situation which left me feeling helpless and hopeless, not a position I was used to! When the sanctuary of my room was reached, the extreme anxiety of my ineptitude possibly leading to a baby's death, found me falling to my knees and shouting at God, If you are real – and I don't believe you are! – tell me what is wrong with this child and I will follow you in the future, no matter what you ask me to do. Bargaining with God, I learned later is not what Christians do, however I felt a sense of release from the tension and anxiety plus a deep peace which was new to me but one which my instinct revealed as being filled with the Holy Spirit.

Walking back down to the hospital and its Pharmacy, my hands picked up medicines which were for the treatment of Meningitis and Heart Failure. I said to God, this could kill the child if this not the correct diagnosis. The response was, 'well I thought you told me that the child was dying anyway!'. The medicines were given, the child lived and grew strong and was discharged home a few weeks later.

Having conveniently forgotten the encounter with God, I was surprised to hear a voice, one morning, calling my name and reminding me of the promise I had made, if God would help heal the child. With a defensive and rebellious reply, I commented that he would need to be real in his relationship with me in the future to enable a meaningful, spiritual, emotional and practical walking together for the rest of my life on earth! Later I realised how arrogant I had been to demand from the creator God to fulfil my needs! He, in his gracious way responded by asking if I had a pen and paper, then to write down each day what my needs were and then after 7 days to see if he had answered the requests. Well of course he had, but still my rebellious, untrusting heart demanded that he made the Bible speak to me because it was like ashes, dead and boring. That weekend I picked up my Bible and read it from the beginning until the end, like a novel, reading right through the night and day, not able to put it down until the last word of the story. It was as though God had given me a glimpse of His Big Plan which involved my surrendering to His will and purpose, learning about His ways, and giving up my agenda based on pride and human spirit of independence from him.

That encounter changed my life for ever, a journey with God which has proved to be blessed, joyful, exciting but also challenging, difficult to the extreme at times. Mountain top and deep valley experiences which have shaped and grown me into a greater spiritual maturity, One which has helped me to acknowledge that my security, significance and self-worth is only to be found in His love for me. The irony is that denominational church upbringing, attending Bible College and serving in a previous Mission Hospital with all its traditional Anglican services etc. had not given me that personal relationship with the Lord Jesus. I had to be steered by God into an inescapable corner of the geographical, practical and spiritual world 6,000 miles from my

British home in order to hear, and be able to receive the gift of the Holy Spirit and bend my knee in gratitude to His Will.

Thanks

I am deeply grateful to all those who have encouraged me to write this book, in particular, those friends and acquaintances encountered over the years who enquired about my 'previous activities' and heard, with some disbelief I learned at a later stage, the details of the Missionary Journey which have given rise to these written memories.

Special thanks go to Stewart Robertson, who assisted me in the purchasing of the technology required to help in the process, but also helped with editing and proofreading the written work from his home in Scotland! Thanks also to Christopher Grizzell for teaching me how to use the technology, to give support backup, and for printing the work along the way. Also to his wife Margaret who released Chris to spend time, effort and money to fulfil this support. Also to Dave Hopwood, for editing and helping me to get my story into the book you now hold in your hands.

Special thanks goes to Dr Penny Jennings, a long term friend who offered to read , rephrase, reorder and give her considerable , professional skills to my meandering writings! I greatly value all the time and effort she has given to this. I hope the experience will encourage her to write her own 'African' story which will be worth reading.

I am thankful also to those on the Call the Midwife Team, particularly Annie Tricklebank and Katie Hamer, who inspired and encouraged me to 'tell my story' for their 2017, BBC televised

Christmas Special programme , set in the 1960s Apartheid years of South Africa. The invitation which followed, to spend a day with the whole team as they filmed a particular episode of their current series, was a wonderfully uplifting experience never to be forgotten.

Very special thanks goes to Dr Jon Larsen who generously allowed me to take photographs and information from his book, KWABAKA, published by Cluster Publications in 2010, and used by the Call the Midwife team for the programme referred to above.

I am indebted to Dr Celia Brown (nee Fiennes) and husband Robert (Bob), for their input into this story which would have been a very different one, set in another country! Sadly Celia died in later years but left a legacy of love in my life which I shall never forget.

To those lovely people who undertook to contribute some of their memories to the relationships part of the book, I want to express great appreciation for your generosity of time, patience and stories which has helped captivate something of the atmosphere of the Barkers and the Charles Johnson Memorial Hospital.

Lastly, but not least, my deeply grateful thanks go to my husband, David, who has spread the word that there was a 'story to be told'. He pushed me into the tight corner that was needed for me to attempt, let alone complete, this piece of work and has proved to be supportive and encouraging when the need was there.

Printed in Great Britain
by Amazon